PASTORAL PREACHING

Pastoral Preaching

EDITED BY

Charles F. Kemp

THE BETHANY PRESS
ST. LOUIS, MISSOURI

Dedicated to

OREN H. BAKER

Pastor, Preacher, Teacher, Friend

ACKNOWLEDGMENTS

Grateful acknowledgment is made to the following for the use of copyrighted material: To Harper & Row, Publishers, Inc., for "Handling Life's Second Bests" from *The Hope of the World* by Harry Emerson Fosdick; to Tidings for "How to Handle Your Load" from *Lift Up Your Heart* by Robert E. Goodrich, Jr.; and to Union Theological Seminary for "Authority and Ministry" from *Union Seminary Quarterly Review* for November, 1958.

TABLE OF CONTENTS

INTRODUCTION

PART I

PREACH THE WORD
Sermons to local congregations

PART II

BRING GOOD TIDINGS
Sermons preached by specialists in pastoral care

INTRODUCTION

THE PURPOSE AND PLAN OF THE BOOK

Phillips Brooks, in his famous Yale Lectures on Preaching, delivered in 1877, made the following statement in his first address:

... the work of the preacher and the pastor really belong together, and ought not to be separated. I believe that very strongly. Every now and then somebody rises with a plea that is very familiar and specious. He says, how much better it would be if only there could be a classification of ministers and duties. Let some ministers be wholly preachers and some be wholly pastors. Let one class visit the flock, to direct and comfort them; and the other class stand in the pulpit. You will not go far in the ministry before you are tempted to echo that desire. The two parts of a preacher's work are always in rivalry. When you find that you can never sit down to study and write without the faces of the people, who you know need your care, looking at you from the paper; and yet you can never go out among your people without hearing your forsaken study reproaching you, and calling you home, you may easily come to believe that it would be good indeed if you could be one or other of two things, and not both; either a preacher or a pastor, but not the two together. But I assure you you are wrong. The two things are not two, but one. ... The preacher needs to be pastor, that he may preach to real men. The pastor must be preacher, that he may keep the dignity of his work alive. The preacher, who is not a pastor, grows remote. The pastor, who is not a preacher, grows petty. Never be content to let men truthfully say of you, "He is a preacher, but no pastor"; or, "He is a pastor, but no preacher."

Be both; for you cannot really be one unless you also are the other.[1]

The Title

When we use the term "Pastoral Preaching" in the title of this volume, we are not thinking of some kind of preaching that is either new or different. Certainly it is not something developed in this generation. Henry Sloane Coffin, in his book *What to Preach*, speaks of five kinds of preaching: Expository Preaching, Doctrinal Preaching, Ethical Preaching, Pastoral Preaching and Evangelistic Preaching. By "pastoral preaching" he means those sermons that develop as a result of the fact that the preacher is also a pastor and a personal friend to his people.[2]

We, too, mean this, but not as something separate and distinct from the other four types of preaching mentioned above. Stated in its simplest terms, pastoral preaching is an attempt to meet the individual and personal needs of the people by means of a sermon. In this sense, a doctrinal sermon, an expository sermon, an evangelistic sermon, or an ethical sermon can also be pastoral. It is a point of view we are advocating, not a separate type or kind of preaching. It is an attempt to take the needs of the people in one hand and the truth of the Christian gospel in the other and bring the two together by means of the spoken word.

Great preachers have always done this. Thomas Chalmers, preaching on "The Expulsive Power of a New Affection," Horace Bushnell on "Every Man's Life a Plan of God," Phillips Brooks on "The Soul's Refuge in God," and Harry Emerson Fosdick on "Six Paradoxes Concerning Trouble" were all doing pastoral preaching. They knew the needs of their people; they also knew the reali-

---

[1] Brooks, *Lectures on Preaching* (New York: E. P. Dutton, 1877), pp. 75-77.
[2] See Coffin, *What to Preach* (New York: Harper & Row, Publishers, Inc., 1926), p. 119.

ties of the Christian faith and had so mastered the techniques of sermon construction and delivery that they were able to bring the two together.

Pastoral Psychology and Preaching

The pastoral psychology movement, which grew out of the impact of the psychological developments of the late nineteenth century, and the pioneer work of such men as Richard Cabot, Russell Dicks, Anton Boisen, Seward Hiltner, and many others, have been basically concerned with pastoral counseling and pastoral care. This, according to the Niebuhr report on theological education, has been one of the most influential movements within the church and theological education of our day.[3]

While the primary emphasis of the leaders in this movement has been on the importance of a face-to-face, or one-to-one relationship, they have all recognized that the pastoral counselor is also a preacher. Seward Hiltner has frequently stressed the fact in his writings that this does not imply two roles, but one. The minister, he says, "has many activities but one role."[4]

The pastoral psychology movement has had a marked influence on preaching at two points: (1) It has made us aware of the needs of people. The very rapid development of the social and psychological disciplines has given us an understanding of human behavior that was not available to any previous generation of preachers. This does not mean that sermons should become psychological discussions. They should not include psychological terms except on rare occasions. Psychology is a resource for preaching, not the subject matter of preaching. As Wayne Oates has put it, the sermons should draw upon psychological wisdom and not be an essay "about" psychology.

---

[3] See Niebuhr, William, and Gustafson, *The Advancement of Theological Education* (New York: Harper & Row, Publishers, Inc., 1957), p. 122.

[4] See Hiltner, *Pastoral Counseling* (Nashville: Abingdon Press, 1949), p. 151.

"Psychological concepts should be understood well enough by the Christian preacher that they can be a part of his preaching without obscuring his main purpose of proclamation of the Christian witness."[5]

(2) A second influence of the pastoral psychology movement on preaching has been a recognition of the need for, and the development of, a trained and qualified institutional ministry. There has always been some form of chaplaincy services in hospitals and penitentiaries, but it was untrained, haphazard, and very limited. One of the really important contributions of the pastoral psychology movement has been the recognition that these vast numbers of people who are being cared for or are forced to reside in the various institutions need a ministry. This would include general hospitals, veterans' hospitals, mental hospitals, reformatories, penitentiaries, schools for the retarded, homes for older persons, etc. The number of people in such institutions would run into the thousands.

With the development of departments of pastoral care in seminaries and clinical training for pastors in hospitals and correctional institutions, there has come a new awareness on the part of the administrators and professional staff of such institutions that a trained pastor has a significant place on the healing and rehabilitation team. Much remains to be done, but the progress thus far has been significant. The number of men engaged in full-time institutional ministry increases each year. In addition to these, there are many more who serve on a voluntary or part-time basis in some institutions.

One of the functions of all such pastors is to conduct worship and to preach. This puts special demands on the preacher.

---

[5]From *The Revelation of God in Human Suffering* by Wayne Oates. © 1959, W. L. Jenkins. The Westminster Press.

The Plan of the Book

In this book we hope to give attention to both of these factors. The first three chapters speak of general principles that provide a background for such preaching. The main body of the book consists of actual sermons which illustrate what pastoral preaching can be. The principle here is obvious: the best way to study preaching is to study sermons.

The book was suggested by Darrell K. Wolfe, director of Bethany Press, as a sequel to another volume, entitled *Life-Situation Preaching,* which appeared in 1956. In some respects the general plan is similar, in others, it is quite different. In the former volume, we included published sermons, both past and present. In this volume most of the sermons are contemporary. With the exception of the sermon by Dr. Fosdick, which was first preached thirty years ago, and the two sermons in the closing section, which were preached more than half a century ago, these sermons are all representative of preaching in our own time. All of the preachers were selected because they have demonstrated unusual capacity in this field.

The book is divided into four sections. In Section I are sermons that were prepared by preachers for specific congregations. Section II is a series of sermons prepared by men who have specialized in pastoral care, and, because of their training and experience, are uniquely able to relate the insights of the pastoral care movement to preaching. In Section III, we have included two sermons prepared for ministers themselves. In the final section, Section IV, we have included two sermons that are representative of great preaching of a previous generation. This makes us aware that pastoral preaching is not new and that much of what they said is still relevant today.

A unique feature of these sermons is that each preacher has been asked to give a brief statement concerning the background of his sermon. Here they tell us something of the congregation, of the purposes they had in mind as they prepared the sermon, and any thoughts they might have about pastoral preaching and their own particular situation.

In order to acquaint the reader with the experience and background of each man, we have included a brief biographical sketch just preceding his sermon.

We would like to express our appreciation to the authors who have contributed what we feel to be a fine selection of "pastoral preaching." We hope their effort will prove to be of value to several different groups:

—to preachers who will be challenged to a new realization of the power of preaching and to new efforts as they try to meet the needs of their people,

—to theological students that they may gain a deeper understanding of their calling as they prepare themselves for the pastorate or the chaplaincy,

—to institutional chaplains that they, too, will gain a greater appreciation of their tasks as they strive to meet the needs of people in special situations,

—to pastors serving on a volunteer, or part-time, basis in institutions in the community that they will have a better understanding of how they can minister on such special occasions,

—to administrators of institutions that they might gain a new appreciation of a religious ministry and of the value of preaching,

—to laymen that they might gain a better understanding of the pastor's task and be lifted and guided by the content of the sermons even as were the congregations that heard them when they were first delivered.

CHAPTER I

AS THE PASTOR SEES HIS CONGREGATION

"When he saw the crowds, he had compassion for them, because they were harassed and helpless like sheep without a shepherd."—Matthew 9:36. Thus the Gospel of Matthew describes Jesus' reaction to the crowd. The Gospel of Mark uses a similar phrase. On this occasion Jesus and the apostles had been seeking a place of quiet across the lake, but the crowd anticipated them and got there first. "As he landed he saw a great throng, and he had compassion on them, because they were like sheep without a shepherd; and he began to teach them many things."—Mark 6:34. So Jesus' message grew out of his response to the needs of the people.

What does the pastor see on a Sunday morning when he looks at his congregation? What is his response? Jesus saw the crowds and was moved with compassion because he saw with such deep understanding. So closely had he identified himself with the people that he felt their problems as his own. As he spoke to crowds, he always saw the individual within the crowd. He noticed Zacchaeus on the edge of the crowd and was aware of both his needs and his possibilities. He singled out Peter and James and John, called Matthew from the place of toll, was aware of a blind beggar by the roadside, of Mary Magdalene, and of the woman by the well. Jesus' preaching was very informal, almost more like a conversation than a sermon. It arose out of human need and was meant to meet human need.

The way the pastor views his congregation will largely
determine his own attitudes, the content of his message,
even his tone of voice. What he sees will be determined
to a large extent by his own insights into human need,
his own understanding, his own compassion. Many people
saw the crowds in Jesus' day, but they weren't moved
with compassion as he was. They didn't have the understanding that he had.

Of course, what the pastor sees on a Sunday morning
will vary with his church. No two congregations are the
same. He will see quite a different group if he is the
pastor of a university church or a small rural congregation; if he is a student pastor with a week-end appointment or the senior minister of a large institutional
church on Park Avenue. Nevertheless, there are some
things that are common to most congregations.

The pastor will see people of all ages, at least this is
usually the case. Some children will be there. Their religion, as yet, is primarily that of their parents, but they
are going through the formative years of life. These are
impressionable years. Their attitudes toward life and
religion are largely being formed now.

Some young people will be there. Much has been
written about adolescents—perhaps too much. Theirs is
a time of transition, often a time of confusion. It certainly is a time of decision. Life's permanent choices
are made during this period, often without much guidance or help—the choice of a life partner, the choice of
a life vocation, and the choice of a life philosophy. These
young people are no longer satisfied with the religion
and the ideas of their parents. They are striving for independence. They want some opinions of their own. The
pastor will be the one to guide them during the time
that their ideas are being formulated and their decisions
are being made. It is a great responsibility.

Some students will be there—many, if it is a university town. They will occupy positions of leadership in the future. They face the responsibility of reconciling their religious faith with the findings of modern science, philosophy, psychology, sociology, and all other branches of learning. This is no easy task. The pulpit should help.

Some people in the congregation are young adults. Theirs is a busy life. They are attempting to establish themselves in business or one of the professions. Their time is consumed with work and activity. They are striving to get ahead, to make payments on the house and the car. They experience one of life's greatest responsibilities—parenthood. This brings a new value to life.

Some of the people are in what is commonly called "middle age." For many this is a time of continued growth, increasing success, significant achievement. For some it is a time of disillusionment. They have not attained the desired position; the promotion went to someone else. They recognize that many of the ambitions of youth will not be realized. Marriage loses some of its romance and children who were welcomed with such anticipation become more of a problem than a pleasure. The pulpit hasn't had too much to say to the middle years.

Some people in the congregation are elderly. According to the national averages, more than 10 percent of any congregation will be over the age of 65, above what government and industry consider retirement age. Actually the number in church usually runs above national averages. All trends indicate that this will continue. It is one of the social phenomena of our day. The United States Department of Health, Education and Welfare issued a publication which pointed out that since 1930, the total population has increased by 30 percent, but the number of persons over 65 has increased by 100 percent.

These people have problems of their own. Our whole cultural pattern makes it difficult for them. The shift

from a rural to an urban society has eliminated many
opportunities for activity for older persons. In previous
generations they could continue to be active on the farm,
in the garden, in household chores. This is a thing of the
past. The mobility of the population means that their families are often far away. The lowering of retirement age
creates not only very real economic problems, but many
personal and emotional ones as well. Housing, limited
income, loss of friends, loss of prestige—all these things
are very real.

Of all these groups, probably the children and the older
persons are most neglected in preaching. A pastor is
aware of young people; he may be overawed by students
(unnecessarily), but he neglects the children and, perhaps, the older persons.

One older person wrote an article in which he com-
mented on this. "What about us?" he asked. "Ministers
are trained to work with young people and they should
be. But is it asking too much to ask ministers to think,
write, plan, preach, and pray in terms of older people?"
He spoke about the sermon specifically.

Sermons about energetic Christian activity have their place
but they leave us lukewarm. We prefer sermons which deal
with peace, comfort, patience, fortitude, the constructive use
of conflict, pain, suffering, spiritual growth, resignation, the
expulsive power of new affections, adjustments to losses, sorrow, anxiety, disability, prayer, and the four things which
abide eternally—faith, hope, love, and resurrection.

We are not interested in frills. . . . We look for relevant
messages in all sermons. But often we old sheep look up and
are not fed. Few ministers deal adequately with our homiletic
needs, and young ministers tend to neglect them almost completely.

All levels of society are in the congregation. This is
probably not as true as it should be. There is some justification for the criticism that Protestantism is a middle-

class church. Let's put it this way: Individuals from all levels of society should be there.

Whether we like to admit it or not, we live in a society of definite classes. Sociologists speak of an upper, middle, and a lower class. These differences are very real—they result in different interests, different thought forms, different moral values. Actually, this is inadequate to describe the true situation, so they further differentiate between an upper-upper class and a lower-upper; an upper-middle class and a lower-middle class; an upper-lower and a lower-lower.

Not many of the upper-uppers will be in our congregations. After all, less than 2 percent of the total population can be so classified. Even so, there may be some. They have their problems, too. It is a false assumption that the comforts and luxuries and advantages that go with material success and social prestige always provide satisfaction. If we could draw an imaginary line down through society and place on one side all those who find life challenging and worthwhile, and on the other side all those who find it futile, meaningless, and empty, we would find that not all those from the upper class are on the meaningful side of the line. As one wealthy woman told her psychiatrist, "If you could convince me my life had some meaning, you wouldn't be hearing this silly story about my nerves."

There may not be many of the lower class in our congregation either, although numerically there is a much greater possibility of these than of the upper-uppers. A little more than 25 percent are classified as lower class. Historically the church has always been concerned about the underprivileged and the dispossessed. Back in the Old Testament the Hebrew law made provision for caring for the poor. Jesus himself told a parable in which the righteous were separated from the unrighteous on the basis of whether or not they had fed the hungry, clothed

the naked, welcomed the strangers, and visited the sick
and the imprisoned.

They are present in our communities. Some have their
names on church rolls. Not many are in our congregations.
They might not be made to feel at home if they were.
Their problems are not only physical and economic,
although these can be very real. Inadequate income results in inadequate housing, insufficient medical care,
improper diet, limited educational opportunities. It also
results in unfortunate emotional and psychological re-
actions. A report of the White House Conference on
Children and Youth states,

There is much evidence that low income and low social
status go together and that children from the lowest level of
American society are looked down upon and discriminated
against. To be shamed and made to feel unworthy, to be told
by word and deed that one is inferior and of little account
interferes seriously with the healthiest development of personality.

These two extremes are among those most neglected
by Protestant churches. To a large extent we have failed
with the upper and lower classes. It is not easy to preach
to both at the same time. They do have different cultural
patterns. They do have different attitudes toward the law,
education, and the church. They see the minister himself
in a different light because they see him in the light of
their own background. Yet both groups are a part of the
pastor's responsibility and when one member of any seg-
ment of society is present, he has a right to be understood.

All levels of intelligence will be present in the church
service. If the pastor could give a mental-abilities test to
all the members of his congregation, he would find a
small group who would be considered gifted, at least
one to five percent, depending on his congregation. There
would be another group who would be considered above
average, or rapid learners. The largest group, of course,
would be in the average range, or from 90 to 110 on an

I.Q. scale. There would also be some below average, the slow learners on the other side of the curve, and a few who would be considered borderline, or retarded.

The New Testament expresses it thus: "To one he gave five talents, to another two, to another one, to each according to his ability." Jesus recognized a long time ago that men have different abilities. Today we can measure those differences with a fair degree of accuracy.

Let's go back to the young people in the congregation. We will select two and call them A and B. A has an I.Q. of 133 that puts him in the top one percent of the population; B has an I.Q. of 69 or 70 that puts him in the bottom one percent. In New Testament terms A has five talents, B has one. In psychological or educational terms A is gifted and B is retarded, or at least borderline.

If both are 12 years of age, then A has a mental age of 16, but B has a mental age of only 8. When they are 15, A will have a mental age of 20, but B will have a mental age of 10. By the time they are adults A will probably have finished college and entered one of the professions, but B will have dropped out of school and will be doing some form of manual labor.

These are not exceptions. One percent seems like a small number until we think of it in terms of the nation, or the community, or the congregation. We have 30,000,000 school children in America. This means 300,000 are in the top one percent. At the other end of the scale the same thing holds true. More than 300,000 retarded children are born each year. If a pastor has a congregation of 500 people, by national averages, he has the possibility of having from 5 to 25 persons who are gifted. These are people with great potential. These people are important for three reasons: (1) Because of the good they can do. If he can challenge them to use their great talents in Christian service, he may be instrumental in helping someone who can make a contribution far greater than anything he himself could have done.

It is a thrilling thought. (2) Because of the harm they
can do. History is full of the tragic records of brilliant
people who had no sense of moral values or concern for
the common good. (3) Primarily because they are persons
and, as persons, have needs like everyone else. They, too,
have a need for acceptance and faith. This does not mean
that the pastor has to become overawed by their presence.
Richard Baxter used to preach a sermon once a year that
was over the heads of the congregation just to show them
what he could do every Sunday if he had to. This is not
what the gifted person needs. He may be more impressed
by a sermon that is quite simple—if it is intelligent and
sincere. Jesus never used words of many syllables; yet
the wisest men of all generations have not exhausted his
meaning.

The retarded person's problem is quite different. He
finds it difficult to understand. He has the same emotional
needs as others—the need for achievement, recognition,
accomplishment, and acceptance—but in our culture he
gets none of these. He comes to church and may not receive them there, either. Yet he, too, is a child of God.
He, too, needs a ministry. He, too, needs to feel that his
efforts and his contribution are worthwhile. It is interesting to note Jesus' emphasis on the value of obscure
acts of service—the widow's mite, the cup of cold water.
These were of significance in the sight of God.

From the standpoint of preaching both of these groups
may be in the same congregation. It is quite possible, in
fact in many cases it is a reality, that the Ph.D., the college
president, the professional man may sit across the aisle
from the man who spent his school years in the slow-
learning class or the school for the retarded. They have
different interests, different backgrounds, a different vocabulary, and different capacities to understand and grasp
ideas, but the pastor must have a message for both of
them.

There are some people in the congregation whose homes are a blessing. After the service during Christian Family Week, when they have heard a sermon on the Christian home, they go home grateful for the home which is theirs. There are others for whom such a sermon creates something of a problem. A Christian home sounds good but they know theirs isn't like that, and it only adds guilt and dissatisfaction. In a country in which a thousand divorces are granted every day, the pastor may be sure that there are people present who are experiencing tension, strain, bitterness, embarrassment, and disillusionment. One authority estimates that if one hundred families are present, at least 33 of them are having adjustment problems serious enough to be causing real difficulty.[1] Of course, this would mean that 67 percent are getting along quite well, for which we are grateful, but all levels of adjustment may be present on any given Sunday.

It has been said that if a man has a good home and a good job, he can stand anything. There is some truth in this. A man's work is almost as important as his home. His standard of living, his freedom from financial concerns depend upon it. More than his economic well-being is involved. His status in the community, his social standing, and his prestige are largely determined by the vocation he follows. Other people will view him differently if he is a lawyer, a doctor, a policeman, a clerk in a store, or a minister of the gospel. His emotional well-being, his mental health will be greatly influenced. If his work is something he enjoys, something in which he takes pride and finds satisfaction, he is most fortunate. If not, if he finds his work boring, if he has no future in his job, if he drags himself to work each day with no more challenge than the thought that it has to be done, then he is most unfortunate.

---

[1]Cf. Edgar Newman Jackson, *A Psychology for Preaching* (New York: Channel Press, Inc., 1961), p. 76.

Richard Cabot, in his classical book, *What Men Live By*, said there were four things that were all-important—work, play, love, and worship. It is significant that a doctor would conclude his list with worship; it is equally significant that he would begin with work. President Eliot of Harvard used to say that Harvard paid him for doing what he would gladly have done for nothing if it had been necessary. Fortunate is the man who shares such feelings toward his job. Some men do. There will be some in the congregation whose work is a real calling, a "vocation" in the true sense of the term.

There are others of whom this is not true. When the minister preaches on the subject, "Every Man's Work a Vocation," or "The Sacredness of Labor," they say, "I wish he had my boss," or "I'd like to have him spend a week at my job and see how sacred he feels it is." Many find themselves in dead-end jobs, with no future; others find themselves in positions that demand more skill or training than they possess, resulting in constant strain; still others find themselves in positions in which they find it difficult to see any value or purpose.

There have been several studies in this area. One study of more than 700 men found the majority were dissatisfied in their work. More than half of them said they would change jobs if they could. Another study of young adults found that three fourths of them would have preferred to be doing something else.

Such people go to work every day but with no challenge and no sense of calling. They are in the congregations, too. Some may need expert vocational guidance. Some need help with personality problems. Probably as many vocational failures come from the inability to get along with others as from lack of ability or training. All men need to see the place of work in life, to recognize that there are satisfactions and discouragements in every field. Some people need to develop new attitudes toward work more than they need a new job. Satisfaction is not always as dependent on having anything we want as in learning to enjoy what we have.

We all need to have a sense of life itself as a vocation. A man's calling is more than the way he makes a living. Amos was a dresser of sycamore trees and a shepherd, but that wasn't his vocation. Paul was a tentmaker and practiced his trade all his life, but that wasn't his vocation. In every congregation there are men whose occupation is in business or in one of the professions, but whose total vocation is vastly more than that. The service they render to the church, to the community, to their friends may be the most important thing they do.

People with all degrees of emotional adjustment may be in the church on Sunday morning. This is not surprising. There are some who find life challenging and real. Every day is a new adventure; every experience is worthwhile. They are able to see themselves objectively. They have problems but they also have insights. They keep themselves under control. They find life pleasant and their sense of humor is contagious.

There are some to whom life is a burden. They may be haunted by a sense of guilt for some wrong, either real or imagined. There is something, perhaps long past, which still festers. It has never been brought out into the open. They pray with the congregation, "Forgive us our debts as we have forgiven our debtors," but they have never gained the assurance of forgiveness.

There may be someone who is confused and perplexed. His life is the 7th chapter of Romans all over again, "I do not do the good I want but the evil I do not want I do." Every pastor has heard people say, "I don't know why I do it. God knows I want to be better."

There may be someone struggling to free himself from the shackles of a binding habit. He sits in church when the pastor speaks of the "good life," but he knows his isn't a good life. He sits there wondering if others know about him, or if he would be embarrassed to try Alcoholics Anonymous. He wonders if it would work for him as others claim it has worked for them, or, he wonders, "This man in the pulpit, would I dare talk to him?"

There may be some who simply have a sense of futility and discouragement. As Mrs. Hoe said in the novel, *If I Had Four Apples*, "God knows I never had anything I wanted out of life." The one word that is so characteristic of many people's lives is the word "meaninglessness." Much of the literature that reflects our culture can be summed up in the one word "emptiness."

All of William James's "varieties of religious experience" may be present and more. There may be some, though not many, who are openly hostile toward religion. As a rule, they are not in church unless forced to come by some relative, or unless they come with the desire to scoff or criticize. There certainly will be some who are skeptical. They sing, "My faith looks up to thee," but they have real doubts about its reality. Webb Garrison says this group is not likely to get much help in church. "There is little incentive for the honest doubter to listen to sermons; his problems are not likely to be helped."[2] There undoubtedly are some who are wistful, seeking, longing, hoping. They may be characterized by the man who came to Jesus and said, "I believe, help my unbelief." They look wistfully to the church and their pastor, hoping to gain a sense of faith, a degree of certainty, and a source of strength. There may be some who are frankly indifferent. They go to church because it's the thing to do, like belonging to the Rotary Club and attending the symphony concerts. The best people in town do it—but they do not have any real sense of need, or any deep appreciation of the meaning of the worship in which they participate, or the claims of Christ upon their lives.

[2]Garrison, *The Preacher and His Audience* (Westwood: Fleming H. Revell Co., 1954), p. 152.

There are others, of course, whose religion is a deep and profound experience. They may not talk about it much, but those close to them know it is real. These are the ones who make a pastor humble, for he knows they demonstrate the things about which he tries to preach.

Here they are. This is the congregation. This diversity is one of the problems of the pastoral ministry. These are areas in which specialists work—and sometimes disagree. Yet the pastor must minister to them all. The pastor must preach to them all—to do so, with meaning and power, is his great privilege and responsibility.

CHAPTER II

THE PASTOR'S UNIQUE OPPORTUNITY

The pastor is not the only one who sees people who are in trouble. The minister is not the only one who helps people with their problems. Doctors, psychologists, psychiatrists, public health nurses, social workers, YMCA secretaries, teachers, school counselors, marriage counselors, vocational counselors, and specialists of all sorts are working with people. They are seeing people in large numbers. Many have long waiting lists. Most of the agencies that specialize in counseling, such as Family Service and marriage-counseling agencies or Child Guidance Centers, do not have sufficient staff to meet the case load.

These people are grappling with real issues. Some of them are doing very effective work. This is one of the encouraging developments on the contemporary horizon. There are large numbers of people who are being helped who would have had no help at all a generation ago.

The story of "man's inhumanity to man" is a long and tragic one. The story of "man's humanity to man" is a very thrilling one that can never really be told. It is taking place in the efforts of those people who have trained themselves to render some particular service in one of the helping professions and thus, in one way or another, are helping people live healthier, stronger, happier, and more effective lives.

Some of these efforts have grown to such proportions that they can rightfully be called movements because they involve and influence so many people. It is one of the most encouraging phenomena of our time. It was only a little more than fifty years ago that Clifford Beers, as a result of his own tragic mental illness, conceived of a program that became the mental hygiene movement. Yet it has already proved a benefit to countless thousands whose conditions have been improved. It has had an impact on medicine, education, social work—on most areas of life. It was as recently as 1907 that Frank Parsons first used the term "vocational guidance," in the annual report of the Vocation Bureau of Boston, of which he was the director. Now there is a National Vocational Guidance Association which numbers its members not in the hundreds but in the thousands. The word "guidance" does not appear in educational literature prior to 1900. Now almost every school has some form of guidance and larger schools have full-time counselors and guidance workers. Charity was once administered by a few kind-hearted, philanthropic-minded persons. Now there are social agencies of many kinds—governmental, religious, and private—which use the services of more than 125,000 social workers. The Family Service movement which arose as one social agency now has a national organization of several hundred agencies and many more professionally trained, full-time marriage counselors. The developments in the field of psychology and psychiatry have created the specialist in medicine, the psychiatrist, and the counseling or clinical psychologist, and have also influenced the thought of all other fields that work with people.

To these movements could be added all sorts of specialists, such as the vocational rehabilitation worker who provides counseling and training for the physically handicapped; the speech therapist who works with those who have trouble with speech; the worker with the retarded and crippled children; the worker with the alcoholic and the delinquent and the aged; etc., etc. All these are specialists of one sort or another who are helping people with their problems.

Counseling crosses most professional lines. It is included as a responsibility of many areas of activity. The doctor, the lawyer, the teacher, the psychologist, the social worker, and many others do counseling—some full-time and some as a part of their other responsibilities. This, of course, would be true of the pastor. Of all the counselors in modern society, however, the minister is the only one who also preaches. He is the only one who appears before his people once a week and speaks to them on the issues of life. This is a unique opportunity.

The fact that he is a preacher can help his work as a counselor. Here in the pulpit he can establish a precounseling relationship. The chaplain of a mental hospital says he feels that the most important thing he does is preach, not because of the content of the sermon, but because here he establishes his identity. The patients know him as a person before he ministers to them as a pastor.

The same is true of the pastor in the parish. When people seek his help as a counselor, or when he calls on them in their homes or in hospitals in a time of need, they already know who he is. They know something of him as a person because they have heard him speak. (Of course, this applies only to those who attend the worship services, but this would be the majority of those who come to see him.) They know something of his attitudes, his point of view, his personality.

We recognize that the pastor's preaching can operate in reverse. It may keep people from coming to him; it may cause people to lose confidence in him. If the preacher is too judgmental, if he lacks sympathy and understanding, if he is too trivial, or if his messages are unrelated to life, then the results can weaken the relationship. One woman, responding to a questionnaire, said, "Our pastor is a good man, and he lives a good life, but I know he does not really know how I feel about not knowing what to do. If he really had to live the way we do, he'd understand better. . . . He does not know what life's problems are. How can he be a real help?" When preaching leaves this kind of impression in the minds of the congregation, then it undermines the possibility of a helpful counseling relationship.

On the other hand, when the preacher, by his message, by his attitude, even by his tone of voice, gives the impression that he understands, that he loves people, that he does have a message of faith and hope, then he can create attitudes of confidence and assurance that are of great value, both in the reception of his sermon and in any later pastoral contacts that may take place. This can be a form of precounseling, especially for those people who come to church conscious of some need. Not infrequently they will say in the pastor's office, "As you were saying in your sermon last Sunday. . . ."

One of the unique things about a sermon is that it is presented in a context of worship. Other people speak to groups. Psychologists and social workers recognize the value of being part of a group; in fact, they go to great efforts to create groups wherein the individual feels accepted and understood. The pastor has a group already available. At its best it is an understanding and accepting group. Even though it falls far short of being the "redemptive community" it was meant to be, the potential is always there and redemptive elements usually are present. To be able to relate people to a group gives a sense of identity, of belonging, of acceptance that in itself produces courage and strength. Part of the task depends upon creating within the fellowship attitudes of understanding and acceptance. When people realize that "all are unacceptable but have been accepted," then they can be more accepting. It also depends upon the preacher and his message. As Edgar Jackson says in *Psychology for Preaching*, "The lonely and distressed person may be integrated with a group through the words that are spoken to the group."

It is important that this is a worshiping group. The sermon is a part of the service of worship. Many people make speeches. Some people even make good speeches. The minister is conducting a service of worship and the sermon is a part of that service.

We cannot take time to discuss the values of worship for personality growth and integration. Suffice it to say that expressions of adoration, praise, thanksgiving, confession, communion, dedication, and commitment, when rightly conceived and really experienced, are the most powerful forces in life. This is a discussion of the sermon. The fact that the sermon is in a context of worship affects both the one who speaks and those who listen. One cannot be trivial or irrelevant (or at least should not be) when his message is a part of a service which includes the great hymns of the church, readings from the Scripture, periods of meditation, and prayer. One listens with a different receptivity when the message is seen as a part of a total experience of worship.

In this setting of worship, the preacher presents his message. The preacher, according to Jackson, is a "healer of souls through the use of words." As he puts it, "He uses words to heal and inspire the souls of men." Men need to be inspired. "Life is continually in need of being lifted up." Here is a great opportunity. Of all those who work with troubled people, the preacher is the only one who can surround his counseling with a philosophy of life; he is the only one who proclaims a gospel; he is the only one who regularly speaks to his people of faith and hope and love.

Men need information as well as inspiration. The minister is the guardian of a body of knowledge that for years has been considered "good news." We are not speaking of mere facts. As one man put it, "If God is, he is not one among many other interesting facts about the universe, like the speed of light. He is the one basic and all-important fact that gives all others their meaning."

The minister, through his sermon, speaks to men of the reality and love of God. He makes real to them the assurance of the forgiveness of sin without which we have no hope. He speaks of life, its meaning, its value, and its eternal destiny. As Wayne Oates has put it, "It is the eternal God in Christ to whom we call attention when we preach, not art or psychology."[1] The preacher gives the people a knowledge of God.

Whenever a discussion on the relationship of preaching and pastoral care is held, someone always raises the question, "How can you reconcile the permissive accepting attitudes of counseling with the judgmental attitudes of prophetic preaching?" No one wants the preacher to tone down his prophetic message. Indeed, some of the problems a pastor faces in the pastoral relationship make him aware of some of the evils of society that need to be condemned. These issues must be faced with courage. The story is told of a certain diplomat who could keep silent in six different languages. Many preachers have learned this diplomatic secret.

Through preaching, the pastor can bring the judgment of the gospel to bear upon the sins of society. Some people may be offended when the preacher touches their

---

[1]Oates, *op. cit.*, p. 11.

prejudices, but others will admire him for his courage. Through preaching, the pastor can warn of the dangers and rebuke the evil in men's lives. There are dangers that need to be avoided. All men need to be called to repentance. This needs to be done. The question is how it is done. When a minister speaks harshly, critically, judgmentally, the listener may wonder what sense of guilt he is compensating for in his own life that he needs to be so hard on others. When his preaching degenerates to continued scolding, it only alienates the people and leads no one to repentance. On the other hand, if the preacher speaks with understanding, gives the impression that he shares the struggles of men, that he is aware of his own finitude and his own involvement, that he is conscious of how difficult it is, he can speak forthrightly against the evils of the day and people will listen. The people will know that while he speaks prophetically against evil, he understands and will work patiently with the one who has done wrong. And while he proclaims with courage the judgment of wrong, his message contains the assurance of divine acceptance and forgiveness and points the way to a newness of life.

Preaching can be a form of preventive religion. It can prevent a lot of problems from arising.

Through preaching the pastor can help people understand and develop those inner resources that make life strong. A few years ago Francis P. Robinson, of Ohio State University, published a valuable book on student counseling. In it he included a chapter with the intriguing title, "High Level Skills of Adjustment." It was his thesis that the counseling movement in education and elsewhere had been primarily corrective and therapeutic in nature. It had emphasized the needs of the neurotic, the delinquent, and the maladjusted. This is true and is, no doubt, the way it should be. Now, he contended, we need to add a new dimension. We should, of course, hold the therapeutic gains we have made but should add another emphasis. We should stress the development of those "high level" skills which enable a person to be more effective, more useful, to live life on a higher level. The church has been concerned about "high level skills of adjustment" for centuries. They are prayer, worship, faith, means of grace, devotional exercises, reading of the Scripture, and acts of service.

Every counselor has seen people who could maintain themselves if they had some inner spiritual resources to fall back upon, to sustain them, to uphold them. As one man has said, "They have no invisible means of support." Through preaching the pastor has the opportunity of making such resources real. Dr. Harry Emerson Fosdick was doing this constantly. If we thumb through the tables of contents of his books of sermons, we find such titles as these over and over again: "Six Ways in Which Modern Man Can Pray," "When Prayer Means Power," "Finding Unfailing Resources," and "Resources for Life's Mastery." Such messages must be both profound and practical. It is not enough to tell men they ought to pray; we must also give them some practical guidance on how to pray. It is not enough to urge men to attend worship services; we must also give them some understanding of the meaning of worship and a knowledge of the God they worship.

Men need all the resources they can get in these days. As Dr. Fosdick has said,

Nine times out of ten, what breaks us down is an external strain plus a sense of internal inadequacy to meet it. A man can keep his morale through almost anything if he has sufficient interior backing, a margin of available strength around his need, a sense of unfailing resource that he can count upon. . . .

These pews and this chancel are full of people who feel like trees in a high wind. Well, the winds are terrific today, and asked what we are anxious about, we naturally say, These tempests. But, you see, what we are really anxious about is our own rootage. . . .

At this point the deepest need in us meets the deepest fact in Chrisianity, and if today these two could be brought together, the result might change the course of many a life here.[2]

Here the pastor supplements the work he does in his office. There he permits the people to drain off their emotions, to come to some understanding of their difficulties, to think through some of their choices. In the pulpit he provides them with the resources of the Christian faith and life which enable them to withstand some of their difficulties, to continue with some of their decisions in spite of discouragement.

Through the pulpit the pastor can challenge people to lives of service. People need not only comfort and reassurance; they also need challenge. Although therapy is not the chief goal or purpose, one can be just as therapeutic as the other. "Whoever would save his life will lose it," is both theologically and psychologically sound. Sermons can help those who are preoccupied with themselves become aware of the needs of others and of great causes to serve. They can make men aware that every life is important, that no one's contribution is insignificant in the sight of God. Thus, if people can be persuaded to give themselves in Christian service, both the individual and the Christian cause are helped.

Preaching, in spite of all its limitations and weaknesses, has done these things. Through the years it has produced results. Sometimes these results have been sudden and dramatic; as when John Wesley sat in the Aldersgate meetinghouse and felt his heart strangely warmed; or when John R. Mott, while still a student, listened to the evangelist Studd speak in a college chapel, and, as a result, made his "life investment decision"; or when Wil-

---

[2]"Finding Unfailing Resources," in *Church Monthly,* Dec., 1941, p. 23.

fred Grenfell, more out of curiosity than conviction, wandered into one of Dwight L. Moody's meetings and was so influenced that he resolved to "try this thing called Christianity to the full or frankly abandon it." Even in these cases, there was no doubt much turmoil going on within the individual previously. Nevertheless, in each case, it was a sermon that brought it to focus.

More than likely, the result is something rather gradual, almost imperceptible. A member of Phillips Brooks's congregation once said of him, "He always makes me feel so strong." Continually to place one's self under such an influence produces an inevitable result. This is the value of preaching. Nothing dramatic may happen as a result of any one sermon, or series of sermons, but the result is there. It is an accumulative effect, like the splitting of a rock. Which blow splits the rock, the first or the last? Neither would have done it alone, but all the blows together produce the desired result.

William James's classic definition of conversion describes it as "That process, gradual or sudden, by which a self hitherto divided, consciously wrong, inferior, and unhappy, becomes unified, consciously right, superior and happy, in consequence of his firmer hold on religious reality." This is the opportunity the preacher has—to speak of religious reality. The results may come gradually or suddenly, as James says, but they come. Preaching is not the only way growth takes place. The pastor uses all the means at his disposal to help his people. Sometimes he sits and listens as they drain off emotion and come to insights. Sometimes he speaks and, from the pulpit, provides them with the information, the inspiration, the guidance, the challenge, the reassurance, and the faith they need. The two functions go together; each strengthens and supplements the other. This is the pastor's unique opportunity: he can both preach and listen, proclaim and counsel. In both, life-changing forces can be set free.

CHAPTER III

IN THE BACKGROUND OF PASTORAL PREACHING

Behind every achievement that is worthwhile there is something in the background; there are many things that made it possible; otherwise, the achievement simply would not have taken place. Behind the scholar's findings, the artist's creation, the scientist's discovery, and the statesman's contributions have usually been years of preparation, personal discipline, persistence of efforts and patience in difficulty.

The same thing is true of preaching. We have spoken in the previous chapter of the values of preaching. What are those things in the background that make it possible,

If a man would do pastoral preaching, first of all he must be a pastor. This is to say the obvious, but it needs to be said. Rufus Jones said, "It is impossible to help anybody with a message until you can in some measure share his life."[1] You cannot speak to people's needs unless you know what their needs are. You cannot know what their needs are unless you go where the people are. You cannot share people's lives from a distance. You cannot understand their needs unless you have time to listen when they come to discuss some of their most perplexing problems and deepest needs.

Real pastoral preaching grows out of a concern for persons, a concern that is so sincere that, as Rufus Jones said, we are willing to share their lives. Jesus looked over the crowds and was moved with compassion because he was concerned. Great pastors have always been concerned about their people.

---

[1] Jones, *The Inner Life* (New York: The Macmillan Company, 1929), p. 49.

No one has expressed it better than Charles Jefferson, in his classical little book, *The Minister as Shepherd*. Speaking of the problem of the church, he said:

Only here and there has it been recognized that the solution of the problem lies in the shepherd—one who shall go where the sheep are, not with a grand declamation, but with a heart that loves and solaces and heals. He must live with the people, think with their mind, feel with their heart, see with their eyes, hear with their ears, suffer with their spirit. He must bear their griefs and carry their sorrows. He must be wounded for their transgressions and bruised for their iniquities. The chastisement of their peace must be upon him, and with his stripes they must be healed. They all like sheep have gone astray, and he must be willing to have laid on him the iniquity of them all. It is the sacrificial note in the ministry which is too often lacking in these later days. The minister has become too much a man of a book. Like the ancient scribes he is a scholar and sometimes a pedant. When the Good Shepherd appeared in Galilee, the contrast between him and the other shepherds was perceived at once. There was a sympathy in Jesus' tone and a gentleness in his touch which proved at once that he was with the people in their sorrows and upward strivings. The chief trouble with the modern church is that in too many localities it has lost contact with the life of the town. It is out of touch with the souls of men in their present perplexities and needs, and hence it cannot influence them. . . . What the world most wants today is shepherding. The world has many comforts, luxuries in abundance; what it lacks is love.[2]

Such a spirit is needed as much today as it was 50 years ago when Jefferson first said it.

This is not an easy task. It can be very time-consuming. Washington Gladden, speaking of the pastor, said, "If he is the kind of man that he ought to be, a great many stories of doubt and perplexity and sorrow and shame and

---

[2]Jefferson, *The Minister as Shepherd* (New York: Thomas Y. Crowell Co., 1912), pp. 101-103.

despair are likely to be poured into his ears."[3] The pastor can't solve such problems in a hurry. Such situations require time, patience, and faith. The problems themselves cannot be described in a hurry. If real solutions are to be found, if real growth is to occur, if real redemption is to take place, some of these people will need to be seen again and again and again. This can put a real strain on the time the pastor has available, for he also has other people to see and other tasks to do.

The limitation of time is only one factor. These tasks also make heavy demands on energy and strength. To quote Gladden again,

There is . . . in every congregation enough of real trouble to tax the minister's resources of sympathy and wisdom. How much there is, in every community, of anxiety and disappointment and heart-breaking sorrow that never comes to the surface, of which the gossiping world never knows anything at all! A great deal of this trouble comes to the minister; he must always be the sharer of many burdens which are hidden from the public gaze. This is just as it ought to be; the pastor has as little reason to complain of it as the doctor has to complain of a multitude of patients. But it is apt to be the most exhaustive part of the pastor's work; the drafts made upon his nervous energy through the appeal to his sympathies are heavier than those which are due to his studies.[4]

At times this sharing of burdens is exhausting—but it is also richly rewarding. It requires all the wisdom and patience a man possesses, but it is a prerequisite to great preaching.

Emerson records an experience that happened to him one winter Sunday when he attended church. Snow was falling outside and was visible through the window. Emerson said,

The snow was real, the preacher merely spectral; and the eye

[3]Gladden, *The Christian Pastor* (New York: Charles Scribner's Sons, 1898), p. 176.

[4]*Ibid.*, pp. 177-178.

felt the sad contrast in looking at him, and then, out of the window behind him, into the beautiful meteor of the snow. He had lived in vain. He had no word intimating that he had laughed or wept, was married or in love; had been commanded, or cheated, or chagrined. If he had ever lived and acted we were none the wiser for it. The capital secret of his profession—namely, to convert life into truth—he had not learned. Not one fact in all his experience had he imparted into his doctrine . . . there [was] not a surmise, nor a hint, in all the discourse that he had ever lived at all.

When a pastor lives with his people and studies the needs of his people, he will be saved from such unreality as Emerson describes.

If a man would do pastoral preaching, he must be a pastor, but he must also be a student. He may never be a scholar in the strict sense of the word, but he must be a student all his life. Sir William Osler, the great physician, used to advise medical students to divide their time equally between books and men. Both are necessary. Studying books helps one understand men; studying persons gives a note of reality to a study of books. Unless one continues to be a student, he is limited to his own wisdom; he has nothing to draw upon but his own experience and observation.

The pastor is basically a theologian. He must be thoroughly familiar with Christian thought and experience. He must ponder the meaning of such words as grace, sin, forgiveness, love, redemption, and salvation, as they apply to the lives of his people. He must interpret these basic needs in language they understand. This is not always easy to do. The story is told (perhaps it is apocryphal) that when Henry James proposed to Elizabeth Jordan, he did so by writing a letter; however, the letter was written in such an involved and complicated vocabulary that she couldn't understand it, and she answered in a note so illegible that he couldn't read it. Sometimes sermons have a similar semantic difficulty. The language of the theologian is not always the same as the language of the man who gets up on Monday morning and goes to the butcher shop, or the accountant's office, or the thousand other places where people spend their time from Monday to Saturday.

The minister must be a student of theology in all of its ramifications, but especially as it relates to the life and the needs of his people.

Seward Hiltner, in a lecture on "The Minister as a Theologian,"[5] described the minister as a man sitting in his study with the great works of the theologians past and present spread before him. Here he is pondering the thoughts of the great minds of all the generations and their meaning for him and his ministry. He also pictured him as a man driving in his car, returning from a home where he has been attempting to minister to the needs of a member of his congregation, and he is pondering the meaning of this experience. In both cases he is a theologian. In both cases he is a student. If he can relate the two experiences and incorporate the relationship into his preaching, he will be doing real pastoral preaching.

One who would do pastoral preaching must also be a student of the Scriptures. He must carry on an intensive and continuous study of the Scriptures, not necessarily as he studied in seminary—hoping to be able to distinguish between the J, D, and P sources for an examination in Old Testament literature; or when he tried to unravel the synoptic problem or come to some conclusion about the authorship of 2 Peter. This is important, and the pastor needs to have a solid foundation in the findings of the biblical scholars. But we are speaking of a study of the Scriptures in which the pastor attempts to understand life and its meaning. He needs to study the Bible so that he will know what it has to say to men who are haunted by a sense of guilt, troubled by doubt, confused

---

[5]Delivered at the Pastoral Care Institute at Texas Christian University, summer of 1961.

about the meaning and purpose of life. As Wayne Oates has said, "The stresses and strains of human suffering bring the Scriptures into bold relief again and again."[6] A prolonged sincere search of the Scriptures is required for the minister to understand life so that he can interpret it to his people. Thurneysen, the European pastor and theologian, expressed it this way,

The Word of God needs to be interpreted and applied in order to bring clarity and direction into the human predicament. We are permitted to be its instrument, provided we first open and dedicate ourselves to the Word. This requires hours, days, years of continuous searching of the Scriptures.[7]

We are not talking about looking for a text for next Sunday's sermon. Most of the preacher's study of the Scriptures should not be for the preparation of some specific sermon, but to saturate his mind and thought with the truth found there, so that when he attempts to deal with some need, the texts are at his fingertips. All great preachers have usually been students of the Scriptures.

Dr. Fosdick was noted as an advocate of topical or life-situation preaching. In his famous article in *Harper's Magazine,* he gave this advice,

Start with a life issue, a real problem, personal or social, perplexing the mind or disturbing the conscience; face that problem fairly, deal with it honestly, and then throw such light on it from the spirit of Christ, that people will be able to go out able to think more clearly and live more nobly because of that sermon.[8]

He advocated beginning with a "life issue," but, in facing it, he drew heavily on the Bible. He might not use a specific text, but might draw on many passages; however, his solution to the problem was almost always found in

---

[6]Oates, *op. cit.*

[7]Thurneysen, A *Theology of Pastoral Care* (Richmond, Va., John Knox Press, 1962), p. 338.

[8]From "What's the Matter with Preaching?" in *Harper's Magazine,* July, 1928.

the Bible. Whether the pastor begins with the Bible and moves to the needs of the people, or begins with the needs of the people and moves to the Bible is not of great concern. In either case, two things have to be present: (1) The pastor has to be aware of what the needs are, and (2) he has to have a mastery of the Scriptures.

The preacher must also be a student of human nature. He can't read all that the psychologists and sociologists are writing, but he can read some. Richard Baxter, Phillips Brooks, Horace Bushnell would have read them if they could. They would have given anything to have understood their people better. All of life was of interest to them. They made every effort to understand human behavior—and, because of their wide experience and sincerity of effort, they did. Psychology is nothing more or less than a study of behavior. The minister must be selective, if for no other reason than the limitation of time, but he dare not neglect any area that will give him a greater understanding of life and the people to whom he must minister.

It is the problems of life that trouble his people. These are the concerns that are in their minds as they sit in the pew. Jackson reports a survey of 4,000 laymen that attempted to discover what their major concerns were.   ✗

The purpose was to find out what people want from their pastors through their sermons. About half of the four thousand queried indicated a concern about intensely personal matters, such as the futility of life, insecurity in personal relations, a haunting sense of loneliness, problems that involve marriage and the proper control of the sex drives, a feeling of inferiority, the effect of alcohol, false ideas of religion and morals, the problem of suffering, as well as the problems of illness and the feelings of guilt and frustration.

Another fourth of those who responded were concerned about family problems, parenthood and child training, infidelity, religious differences, and other problems that were symptoms of tensions in human relations. The remainder and relatively small minority were concerned about social, community, and the more traditional religious problems.[9]

If the preacher is to deal with such subjects as these, he dare not do it superficially or artificially. One of the problems of pastoral counseling is that people come to the pastor expecting quick and easy solutions. There are none. This is also a danger of such preaching. The pastor is tempted to oversimplify some very deep and real issues. These are problems that cause men to lie awake nights, that destroy their happiness, that divide homes, that create a feeling of estrangement between man and God. No one has a right to attempt to speak on such issues without thoroughly studying the thought of those who have had wide experience and have conducted extensive research on such problems.

When a pastor does study human nature, combines it with a thorough knowledge of the Scripture and relates it to the great affirmations of Christian thought, then he can preach with the assurance that he can help.

How does the pastor find time for such study? There is only one answer. It requires discipline, planning, patience, and commitment. He must establish some priorities on his time and energy so that such study will be done. The vastness and significance of the task requires it.

We expect this in other fields. Paul, in his day, compared his efforts to those of the athletes of that time, who disciplined and trained themselves to win an earthly crown. A sports magazine tells of Ben Hogan's preparation for a golf tournament when he was at the height of his career. He would arrive at the site of the tournament weeks in advance. He would study the course meticulously. He would practice for hours until his hands were blistered and raw. Then he would take a club to his hotel room and practice at night. Every shot with which he was confronted in competition he had made 100 times before.

---

[9]Jackson, *op. cit.*, p. 75. Used by permission.

He was a dedicated person.

This is true in other fields. Fred Eastman, in a biographical sketch of Abraham Lincoln, describes the occasion of his famous "lost speech," when he reached such heights of eloquence that even the reporters forgot to take notes. He arose awkwardly to his feet, his suit wrinkled from a long train ride, a very unassuming, almost pathetic figure. But he spoke with such sincerity and earnestness that the audience was captivated. Such an incident doesn't just happen. There is always much in the background. Eastman described it this way: "All his defeats, all his reading of the Bible, Shakespeare, Byron, and the lives of Washington and Franklin, all his efforts to discipline himself in the art of expression, now come to fruition. He is a man of power. In his heart the heart of the people beats."[10]

The pastor must submit himself to the same kind of discipline so that it can be said of him, "In his heart the heart of the people beats."

Study alone is not enough. Anyone who really tries to meet the needs of the people and speak on such issues as we have been mentioning here realizes his own inadequacy. For this reason he must be not only a student but must be also a man of prayer.

L. J. Radcliffe said, "It is just because we need a wisdom and a power greater than our own that we cry out in prayer."[11] Charles Whiston, in his book *Teach Us to Pray,* includes a chapter for the minister. In this section he says, "In a special way, therefore, because of our acceptance and commitment to the vocation of the Christian ministry, we clergy must be men of prayer. We dare not attempt to do His work without the preparation and dedication of prayer."[12]

To relate it to our theme of preaching, this prayer

---

[10]Eastman, *Men of Power,* Vol. IV (Nashville: Abingdon Press, 1939), p. 59.
[11]Radcliffe, *Making Prayer Real* (Nashville: Abingdon Press, 1956), p. 62.
[12]Whiston, *Teach Us to Pray* (Boston: Pilgrim Press, 1949), p. 226.

should take several expressions. It should be a prayer of gratitude for the high privilege of being part of such a great tradition and sharing in such a significant calling. This is a privilege for which all should be grateful. It should be a prayer of confession, for every pastor knows that no matter how hard he tries, he falls far short. It should be a prayer of intercession for the people to whom he preaches—personal, individual intercession. When John Fredric Oberlin was carrying on his great ministry in the Vosges Mountains of France, he used to pray an hour a day for his people, by name. His people knew it and passed his house in silence because they knew he was praying for them. "A deep spirit of intercessory prayer, a sincere love for others, a creative awareness of God's power and willingness to help all His children—these are the necessary conditions of spiritual influence."[13]

It must be a prayer of dedication and commitment. Jesus prayed, "For their sakes I sanctify myself." For their sakes, for the sake of those in his congregation, the pastor dedicates himself.

Only with such spiritual resources can the pastor hope to meet the needs of persons. Only when he is "strengthened with power by His spirit in the inner man" can he withstand the temptations of both success and failure. Only thus does he have the motivation for continued discipline.

In the Gospels we read that the disciples, seeking Jesus a great while before day, found him in a desert place, by himself alone. Thus he began the day's ministry. Again we read that when the day's activities were over, he withdrew to a place apart and prayed.

What took place in these moments of solitude, we do not know. We do know they were there in the background of his ministry. These, too, are our resources as we attempt to minister in his name.

---

[13]Radcliffe, *op. cit.*, p. 80.

PART I

Preach the Word

Sermons to local congregations

*". . . it pleased God through the folly of what
we preach to save those who believe."*
—1 Corinthians 1:21

*". . . preach the word, be urgent in season and
out of season, convince, rebuke, and exhort,
be unfailing in patience and in teaching."*
—2 Timothy 4:2

Pastors since the days of the letter to Timothy have been admonished to "preach the word." But the word must be preached to specific congregations, at a specific time in history, occupying a specific place geographically and culturally. Congregations are different. Like people, they have their own personalities. Different congregations have different backgrounds, interests, vocational pursuits, and cultural patterns. All of the sermons in this section were prepared by pastors with the needs of specific local congregations in mind. The congregations represent a wide cross section of American life. Some of these are urban in nature. One is located at the heart of a large metropolitan center. Some are from smaller communities. Some are suburban. One represents a university community where students and professors are very prominent in the congregation. One is a church located in the open country. In these sermons we have an example of how pastors can speak to the needs of their people today.

Biographical Sketch

HARRY EMERSON FOSDICK

A volume like this would be incomplete unless it included a sermon by Dr. Fosdick. More than any single individual, he has influenced the pattern of contemporary preaching. Probably more than any individual, he has been able to incorporate the insights of psychology and a counseling ministry into a vital pulpit ministry.

So effective has he been, and so widely has he been quoted and copied, that it is surprising to find that preaching was very difficult for him; in fact, he says, "at the start . . . exceedingly painful." For a long time he literally struggled with the problem of preaching. He was dissatisfied with the prevailing mode of expository preaching because it did not seem to get to the real needs of the people; he was equally dissatisfied with the alternative suggested by many—topical preaching. He said that the former did not meet the needs of the people who came to his church; the latter seemed little better than lectures on contemporary topics of interest. It was in the relationship of preaching and pastoral work that he found his answer. In his own words, "So I floundered until personal counseling gradually led me into an approach to preaching which made it an exciting adventure."[1]

This relationship did not come suddenly. It was a gradual growth resulting from his enlarging ministry on the one hand and his persistent, almost intense search on the other, to discover a more effective method and philosophy. Again in his own words, "Little by little . . . the vision grew clearer. People came to church on Sunday with every kind of personal difficulty and problem flesh is heir to. A sermon was meant to meet such needs; it should be personal counseling on a group scale."[2]

He said that the place to begin was with people's needs, needs that were "puzzling minds, burdening consciences, distracting lives." This, in turn, made the Bible become alive. He found that he could not deal with crucial life issues without utilizing the Scripture. According to Dr. Fosdick, this

---

[1]Fosdick, *The Living of These Days* (New York: Harper & Row, Publishers, Inc., 1956), p. 93.
[2]*Ibid.*, p. 94.

kind of preaching is not so much thinking "for the people" as it is "cooperatively thinking with them." However, he always saw preaching, to use an old homiletical phrase, as "preaching for a verdict." This is the difference between a sermon and a lecture. A lecture is a subject to be discussed and a sermon is an object to be attained.

The preacher's business is not merely to discuss repentance but to persuade people to repent; not merely to debate the meaning and possibility of Christian faith, but to produce Christian faith in the lives of his listeners; not merely to talk about the available power of God to bring victory over trouble and temptation, but to send people out from their worship on Sunday with victory in their possession. A preacher's task is to create in his congregation the thing he is talking about.[3]

Dr. Fosdick's ministry was marked by great success in terms of the crowds who came to hear him preach and the thousands more who heard him on National Vespers from coast to coast, but his concern was with the individual. If the preacher is really dealing with the problems of the people in the pew, Dr. Fosdick says, then on any given Sunday the preacher may have the assurance that through that sermon "he might help at least one individual." Describing his own practice and his own purpose, he said, "My silent prayer rose each Sunday before the sermon started: 'O God, some one person here needs what I am going to say. Help me to reach him!'"[4]

This sermon was preached thirty years ago, but because he spoke to actual needs, universal needs, it applies as much today.

[3] *Ibid.*, p. 99.
[4] *Ibid.*, p. 100.

Handling
Life's Second Bests

WE ARE CONCERNED TODAY about a factual personal problem so nearly universal in its application that we need not be bothered by its exceptions: namely, that very few persons have a chance to live their lives on the basis of their first choice. We all have to live upon the basis of our second and third choices. To one who reads biography this comes to be so much a matter of course that he takes it for granted.

Whistler, the artist, for example, started out to be a soldier and failed at West Point because he could not pass in chemistry. "If silicon had been a gas," he used to say, "I should have been a major-general." Instead, he failed in soldiering, halfheartedly tried engineering, and then tried painting—with such remarkable results as one sees in the portraits of his own mother, Miss Alexander, and Carlyle.

Let us approach this unescapable human problem of handling life's second-bests by way of one of the most impressive exhibitions of it in history. In the sixteenth chapter of the Book of the Acts, in the record of Paul's journeys, we read this: "When they were come over against Mysia, they assayed to go into Bithynia; and the Spirit of Jesus suffered them not; and passing by Mysia, they came down to Troas. And a vision appeared to Paul in the night: There was a man of Macedonia standing, beseeching him, and saying, Come over into Macedonia, and help us. And when he had seen the vision, straightway we sought to go forth into Macedonia, concluding that God had called us to preach the gospel unto them."

So simple and succinct is this narrative that one would little suspect that we are dealing with one of the most significant events in human history. Here Christianity passed over from Asia into Europe. It was a momentous day when Columbus set sail from the shores of Spain or Vasco da Gama discovered the sea route to the Indies, but could even such events be more pregnant with consequence than the day when Paul carried Christianity out of Asia, in a few centuries to be overrun by Mohammedanism, through Troas into Macedonia and so to Europe, where Christianity was going to have its chance? But Paul had not planned to go to Europe. That was a second choice. Paul had planned to go to Bithynia. "They assayed," it reads, "to go into Bithynia." And no wonder, for Bithynia was one of the richest provinces of Asia Minor, and to have carried Christianity there would have been a triumph indeed.

Moreover, we may be sure that if Paul wanted to go into Bithynia he wanted to go very much and tried to go very hard, for Paul was never a half-way man. And he could not go; the way was blocked; his plan was broken. We read, "The Spirit of Jesus suffered them not," but that is only another way of saying that some circumstance blocked their course. It must have seemed to Paul lamentable at first. I picture him arriving on the shores of the Aegean, saying, I wanted to go to Bithynia and here I am in Troas! And lo! through Troas a way opened to the pre-eminent ministry of his career. Paul rendered his most significant service with the left-overs of a broken plan.

Wanting Bithynia and getting Troas, how familiar an experience that is! But to take Troas, the second-best, the broken plan, the left-over of a disappointed expectation, and make of it the greatest opportunity we ever had, how much less familiar that is! Yet, as one reads the story of human life, one sees that powerful living has always involved such a victory as Paul won in Troas over his own soul and his situation.

When a career has at last been finished and the halo of well-deserved reputation now hangs over it so that one cannot think the name without thinking of some high enterprise with which the name is indissolubly associated, then in the glamour of that retrospect we are tempted to forget that almost always the turning point of the career is the experience that Paul had—getting Troas when he wanted Bithynia.

When, for example, we think of Phillips Brooks, we think of spiritual ministry, a great personality pouring his soul out with abundant power upon the people. Of all the letters that Phillips Brooks received, it is said that he cherished most this one from a small tailor shop near Copley Square in Boston: "Dear Mr. Brooks: I am a tailor in a little shop near your Church. Whenever I have the opportunity I always go to hear you preach. Each time I hear you preach I seem to forget all about you, for you make me think of God." Nevertheless, remember that Phillips Brooks did not plan to be a preacher. He planned to be a teacher. That was his Bithynia. As soon as he graduated from college he plunged into his chosen profession of teaching and he failed. He failed completely. Listen to young Brooks writing about his scholars as he is failing: "They are the most disagreeable set of creatures without exception that I have ever met with. . . . I really am ashamed of it but I am tired, cross and almost dead, so good night." Listen to Phillips Brooks after he had failed and been dropped from his position: "I don't know what will become of me and I don't care much"; "I shall not study a profession"; "I wish I were fifteen years old again. I believe I might make a stunning man: but somehow or other I don't seem in the way to come to

much now." Listen to Phillips Brooks's father, concerned
about his son, so humiliated that he will not talk even
with his friends: "Phillips will not see anyone now, but
after he is over the feeling of mortification, he will come
and see you."

There is a sense in which Brooks never recovered from
the disappointment. At the flower of his career he came
down once from the office of President Eliot of Harvard
white as a sheet and fairly trembling because he had
declined what he knew to be his last opportunity to become a teacher. He wanted Bithynia and he got Troas
but through Troas he found the door into a service that
if he had lived a hundred lives he might never have
found again.

Or consider Sir Walter Scott. We think of him as the
novel-writer whose stories charmed our youth so that for
many years some of us would have voted Ivanhoe the
best tale ever told. Sir Walter, however, did not want
to be a novelist; he planned to be a poet, but Byron's
sun rose and dimmed his lesser light. "Byron hits the
mark," he said, "where I don't even pretend to fledge
my arrow." Then he turned to writing novels, so ashamed
that, as you know, he published the first of them anony-
mously. He did not want anyone to know that he was
writing novels. He wanted Bithynia; he got Troas and
through Troas an open door to the best work he ever did.

Is there anybody here who has not wanted Bithynia
and gotten Troas? We older people watch the youths
come up, as we did, with their ambitions and plans for
Bithynia and we wonder what they will do when they
face the unescapable experience. When they are shut out
from some Bithynia and land in Troas, will they know
how to handle that? Will they have the spirit and attitude
and the technique to make of it their finest chance? And
since it is so unescapable a problem, we well may ask
what it was in Paul that enabled him to turn his defeat
into victory.

For one thing, his religion entered in. Whatever else was shaken when he got to Troas, his conviction still was there that God had a purpose for his life, that if God had led them to Troas there must be something in Troas worth discovering, that God's purposes included Troas just as much as Bithynia, that God never leads any man into any place where all the doors are shut. Paul's religion entered in.

It is in just such situations as this that one can tell how much real religion a man has. We hear a man reciting a familiar creed: "I believe in God the Father Almighty, Maker of heaven and earth," but no matter how serious he may seem about it you cannot tell from that alone how real it is to him. You hear a man singing,

> He leadeth me: O blessed thought!
> O words with heavenly comfort fraught!
> Whate'er I do, where'er I be,
> Still 'tis God's hand that leadeth me.

But however much in earnest he may seem you cannot tell from that alone how deep it goes with him. When, however, you see a man who, wanting Bithynia, gets Troas and, still certain that there is a purpose for his life, takes a positive attitude toward Troas as if to say, If God has led me here there is something worth while here to do, you know that that man's religion is practically operative. If, therefore, Paul had merely said what he did say, "To them that love God all things work together for good," we might have cocked suspicious eyebrows at him, thinking that that proposition is extraordinarily difficult to prove. What is impressive about Paul is that whenever he did land in a disappointing Troas, and he landed in a good many of them, he did so effectually love God that he *made* all things work together for good. Paul's religion meant to him a positive faith about life and a positive attitude toward life so effective that watching his career is again and again like watching the Battle of Marenog—in the morning an obvious defeat, in the afternoon a resounding victory.

Consider a modern counterpart of Paul, Adoniram Judson. When Judson was a young man he gave himself to missionary service and his ambition centered on India. That was his Bithynia. When at last he reached India they would not let him in. The East India Company would not allow him to stay and the governor told him to take the first ship back to America. For a year he labored to open the doors of India and they were bolted shut. So he turned to Burma. That was his Troas, unknown, untouched Burma. Can one suppose that through all that humiliation and disappointment Judson could always see the leadership of God? Of course he could not; he was human. Can anyone suppose during those months that he lay in the prison of the Emperor at Ava and Oung-Pen-La he could always see evidences of the divine purpose? Of course he could not; he was human. But he did so handle the affair in Burma that the doors began to open until no well-instructed man today can think of Burma without thinking of Adoniram Judson, or think of Adoniram Judson without thinking of Burma; and when the consequence began to appear he could look upon his life in retrospect as though it had been planned of God. To live your life through—not argue it through; that never is sufficient—to *live* your life through into the conviction that there is an eternal Purpose with which a man can ally himself is one of the finest achievements of the human spirit.

Altogether the most thrilling story in the Old Testament is on this theme. One day in Palestine we stopped our automobile by the roadside and ate our lunch at Dotham where long ago Joseph had been sold by his brethren. Still the camel trail goes up from across Jordan, and then runs down to the coast cities and so to Egypt. Now Joseph, stolen from his home, betrayed by his brethren, dropped into a pit, sold to Midianite slave-dealers, made a manservant in a household in Egypt, lied about by his master's wife and put in prison—can one suppose that during all that humiliation and disgrace he could see where God was taking him? Of course not. But he so kept his faith and handled his life that the doors opened into the biggest business of his career, and when at last those penitent and frightened brethren stood before him, you remember what he said: "I am Joseph your brother, whom ye sold into Egypt. And now be not grieved, nor angry with yourselves, that ye sold me hither: for God did send me before you to preserve life. . . . So now it was not you that sent me hither, but God."

Such was Paul's feeling as he looked back on the day he missed Bithynia and found Troas, and such will be ours if in Troas we will let our religion enter in.

In the second place it was not simply Paul's religion that enabled him to win this victory but the fine fruit of his religion, his care about people.

The trouble with so many of us when we land in Troas is that we begin to pity ourselves. Paul could have done that. He could have started the process we indulge in—"ifing."

If I had not missed Bithynia; if my plans had not been broken, if if! I have given up everything for Jesus Christ. I could today be one of the great rabbis of Jerusalem saluted in the market place. I have given it all up for Christ. I spent a long time in Arabia thinking through the gospel. I have been fourteen years in a trying, difficult, unrecognized ministry in Cilicia, at odds even with my Christian brethren because once I persecuted them. And now, when I am beginning to get on a good footing with my fellow Christians, with Barnabas and a few others trusting me, I have come up through Asia Minor on a preaching mission. See what they have done to me. They stoned me and left me for dead in Lystra. Even after that, all I asked was that I might have a chance to get into Bithynia and do some good work, and now I cannot; I am foiled; my plan is broken.

How easy it would have been for Paul in Troas to feel sorry for himself.

Upon the contrary, he at once began thinking about other people. He wondered if there was not someone who might be better off because he had landed in Troas. He had not been there a night before he saw a man from Macedonia saying, Come over and help us. It was Paul's unselfishness, his generosity, his magnanimity that opened the doors for him in Troas.

Once there was a man named William Duncan who gave himself to the missionary cause and in time was sent by his board to a little Indian island off Alaska called Metlakatla. It was an unlikely Troas for a young man to land in who had doubtless dreamed of some Bithynia, for those Indians were a poor, ignorant, miserable tribe, and their morals were vile beyond description. Dean Brown of Yale, however, who visited Metlakatla after William Duncan had been there about forty years, makes this report, that you will find every Indian family in a separate house with all the decent appointments of home life, that you will find a bank, a co-operative store, a saw-mill, a box factory, and a salmon cannery run by Indians in profitable industry, that you will find a school where Indian boys and girls learn to read and write and think and live, and a church where an Indian minister preaches the gospel of eternal life and an Indian musician, who once was a medicine man playing a tom-tom, now plays a pipe organ, and a congregation of Indians sing the great hymns of the church to the praise of Almighty God—and all because a man named William Duncan, landing in Troas, cared enough about people to find there the chance of his life!

My friends, there is nothing in that spirit or consequence that cannot be transferred to our lives. We are all in Troas. Just as at Sebastopol each heart thought a different name while they all sang Annie Laurie, so when today we say "Troas" each one of us thinks of some situation we would not have planned to be in. There is only one way—love. Was it not George Macdonald who said: "Nothing makes a man strong like a cry for help"? You walk down the street utterly fatigued, so tired that you would like to lie down on the curb and go to sleep, and suddenly there is a cry; there has been an accident; a child is hurt; and you never will remember how tired you are until it is all over. Nothing makes a man so strong as a call for help.

A mother is completely fatigued. She has been telling her friends for weeks that there is nothing left of her, and then a child falls ill and needs her. Week after week, by night and day, she stands by and never thinks of being tired. Nothing makes a man strong like a call for help.

It would be strange indeed if there were not some young men and women here not altogether dull to the dangers of our civilization, not altogether blind to the possibility of losing it, thinking that perhaps there is something in them that might help build a more decent world for human children to be born in. That is their strength. Nothing makes a man so strong as a call for help. And the trouble is that when we get into Troas we pity ourselves; we miss that man from Macedonia, saying, Come over and help us.

Indeed, so true is this principle of life that it holds good of even small excursions into Troas. When annoyances and irritations come, when one is lied about and hated and denounced, there is only one way out—goodwill. You remember Edwin Markham's lines:

> He drew a circle that shut me out—
> Heretic, rebel, a thing to flout.
> But Love and I had the wit to win:
> We drew a circle that took him in!

If in the midst of life's harassments and irritations one has grace enough to do that, he sometimes will find in that very difficulty his choicest opportunity for usefulness.

This, then, is the conclusion of the matter: that because Paul had these two elements in his life, as soon as he landed in Troas his imagination was filled, not with defeat but with victory. Coué was right that it is the imagination which makes or unmakes us. If you put a thirty-foot plank as high as a cathedral tower hardly anybody can walk it, and it is not because the physical difficulties are greater than they would be on the ground but because one's imagination keeps picturing him falling off. So when we get into Troas we think we are defeated. I wanted Bithynia, we say; I have got Troas. So we think defeat, we say defeat, we imagine defeat, and we are defeated. But as soon as Paul landed in Troas he saw an open door, a beckoning man, a new chance, and a successful issue.

What helped him most, I suspect, was that his thought went back, as it so habitually did, to the cross of his Master. That was a Troas to land on! What a Bithynia it would have been if his people had accepted Jesus as Messiah! And now, shut out from that Bithynia, he came to his Troas, his Calvary, and he so clothed it with the purpose of God and the love of man that

> All the light of sacred story
> Gathers round its head sublime.

He took a very hard thing and he made of it a triumph.

Biographical Sketch

CARLYLE MARNEY

DR. MARNEY is the pastor of the Myers Park Baptist Church, in Charlotte, North Carolina. He went there from a significant ten-year ministry at the First Baptist Church, Austin, Texas. Prior to that, he served several churches in Kentucky.

He holds the A.B. degree from Carson Newman College and both the Master of Theology and Doctor of Theology degrees from Southern Baptist Theological Seminary. He has traveled widely and has served in various positions, both denominational and interdenominational, including the Study Committee of the World Council of Churches and the Theological Commission of the Baptist World Alliance, and as a trustee of *The Christian Century*. For several years he served as Professor of Christian Ethics and Visiting Professor of Homiletics at Austin Presbyterian Seminary.

Dr. Marney has published several books. The titles of his publications reveal his wide range of interests: *Faith in Conflict, Beggars in Velvet, These Things Remain, Structures of Prejudice.*

He is recognized as one of the most effective preachers of our day. His influence has extended far beyond the local congregation. He has preached or lectured on more than fifty campuses, including the Battell Chapel at Yale, Memorial Chapel at Harvard, and Rockefeller Chapel at the University of Chicago. He has served as Preaching Missioner to numerous Army and Air Force Bases, and was sent on an assignment to the Far East Air Forces. He was Peyton Lecturer at Southern Methodist University, Cunningham Lecturer at Austin College, Wells Lecturer at Texas Christian University, and Convocation Lecturer for Summer Institutes at Princeton Theological Seminary and Union Theological Seminary.

Dr. Marney reads widely in many fields and all of this background of study and experience finds expression in his preaching. The bulletin of Pastoral Psychology Book Club described him as a man who was "equally at home in the worlds of philosophy, psychology, sociology, and ethics," but also as one who "successfully integrates the contributions of the social sciences with a profound Christian understanding" of our most pressing contemporary problems. These words were written in connection with his recent book, *The Structure of Prejudice*, but they can be applied to his preaching as well, as is evident in the sermon that follows, which deals with a common problem today.

Dr. Fosdick has said regarding preaching that a sermon should not be a "dogmatic monologue but a cooperative dialogue in which the congregation's objections, questions, doubts and confirmations are fairly stated and dealt with."[1]

One problem of much contemporary preaching is that it never achieves this goal of a dialogue that confronts and involves the minds of those in the pew.

Dr. Marney has conducted a unique program in his church which fosters this dialogue and gives any who wishes a chance to pursue the thought of the sermon. On a Sunday evening he invites all who are interested to meet at the church to discuss the sermon of the morning. At this time they have a chance to raise questions or objections, to seek further clarification. This takes real courage, but it certainly makes it possible to relate the sermon to the life of the people, for it enables them to verbalize their own feelings about it and gives the pastor a chance to apply the universals about which he speaks to individual and specific questions and problems.

---

[1] Fosdick, *For the Living of These Days*, p. 97.

In the Meantime

MOST OF LIFE IS LIVED *in the meantime*. If a man does not learn to live in the meantime, he is less than half alive.

All ages are restless ages to the people who live in them. All times are critical to people who have problems. All roads are weary roads when we have too far to walk. People do not like to wait. This is a badge of our immaturity.

People have always had to live waiting for something. Usually, they wait for peace. They wait for sons to come home from World War III, or brothers to return from World War II, or fathers to get out of World War I. Grandmothers waited for grandfathers to come home from Cuba and the Spanish War; Great-grandmothers waited for the release of the prisoners from Rock Island and Richmond and Memphis. Great-great-great-grandmothers waited for the Revolution to grind to an agonizingly slow end. People have always had to live waiting for something: usually peace, or daylight, or recovery of sanity, or husbands to come home, or sons to get well.

People stand in line most of their lives. They wait for a pass, or they wait for a friend, or a break, or payday, or death. They wait for quitting time, or the installments to be paid out, or the doctor to come. They wait for prosperity, or independence, or comfort, or restoration. They wait for their youth to come back, or for power, or for revival. They wait for the Republicans to get in or out, for stocks to go up or down, for the mailman; or sometimes, when they are pastors, they lean back against the corridor wall of the hospital with a fellow and wait for the undertaker to come. Practically all of life is lived "in the meantime"—some meantime or some other meantime. If a man does not learn to live in the meantime, he finds himself less than half alive.

What meantime?

It is that valley which extends from Sunday night when he goes away until Friday when he comes home. It stretches from plane to hotel to dreary restaurant fare and second-run movies and time-killing rented TV—until he gets home again. The meantime? It is the interminable stretch between letters; the agonized pacing of the corridor outside the wing marked "Surgery." It is the long journey from an old home to a new home; it is the dusty journey made after all his friends have gone into the beyond ahead of him.

The meantime?

It is the endless term with old magazines in the room marked "Waiting"—"White Only" where a man listens for the arriving loved one or awaits the beginning of a dreaded journey or the turn in the chair with the old doctor or the new specialist or the laboratory report. The meantime is the dreaded miles at night between a man and home base when the white line stretches out interminably in the headlights, and he is hypnotized by fatigue. It is the all-night vigil between the day his child was well and the day he will be well again. Most of life is meantime.

How can he live when his heart is somewhere else? How can he make it when his dreams have no prospect of coming true? How can he work when his hope is so distant from its consummation? How can he grow in this captivity? How can he endure the silence when he longs for strident sound and the singing voices? How can he see in this darkness when his eyes were made for light? How can he live in the meantime?

Long before Christ, Jeremiah found out about meantimes and how to live in them. All the way from Ana-
thoth, his boyhood village where he had a pastorate with
disastrous consequences to himself, down to his eventual
stoning by his fellow countrymen in Egypt, Jeremiah had
reason to know about meantimes. So he wrote a letter, a
very famous letter, and sent it down to Babylon for the
exiles to read: He said it was a letter from God for captives: "Thus says the Lord of hosts, the God of Israel,
to all the exiles whom I have sent into exile from Jerusalem to Babylon:"—to thousands of Jews, huddled in
Babylon in camps on the banks of canals and artificial
rivers, nine hundred miles and a thousand days from the
noises and agonies of Jerusalem's fall. Their memories of
their dying still scream in their ears; their brains reel and
are made stupid by the brazen sounds of pagan worship.
Their spirits are overwhelmed by the colossal might of
Babylon's military which had smashed them, on horse-
back, fighting in ranks, riding wheeled instruments of war.
They are still befuddled by the clanging chaos of Jerusalem's fall; bogged down now in foreign mud; desolate
of any hope for a relieving column to rescue them; prom-
ised relief by prophets they knew to be rumor mongers;
false hope slipping off into false despair day after day.

Their captors call "Sing us a song!" But how can they
sing the songs of the Lord in a strange land? How can
they keep the cunning of their skills for revolt alive? How
can they forget the debacle that marked the fall of the
city? How can they forget their babies crushed in the
press at the gate of the city? And how can they hope
when no one can set a limit to their hurting? How can
they live, in the meantime?

Jeremiah found out and wrote it down, and one day,
months later, one of Israel's greatest documents, the letter from God by Jeremiah, was smuggled in and passed

from hand to hand, elder to elder, camp to camp. It began from God, and it said, when they are caught, captive, bound, and unable to pass: "Build houses and live in them; plant gardens and eat their produce." In the meantime of captivity—do the everyday jobs—*do the next thing! There is healing in the performance of the prosaic.*

More than a few times I have turned with some friend from the cot where death has just slacked a jaw, or from the hearth where death has sent a telegram, to find a watering pot or a broom to use. "Miss Myrtle, your flowers are dry and brittle, you haven't watered them." Or, "Ruby, let's *work!*" Sometimes the only thing to do is *work*—anything if it's done like an automaton—no thinking—just *work*. Or sometimes I say, "Let's make the lists now of all we have to call." Or I say, "Let's gather up the things now." The next thing! Sometimes it's all one can do because it's all there is—and Jeremiah says there is a healing in it. Do the next thing!

And in the meantime: "Take wives and have sons and daughters; take wives for your sons, and give your daughters in marriage, that they may bear sons and daughters." In the meantime, there is a fellowship to be considered. The Lord advised the Jews to see to their wives and sons and daughters in this foreign land. None of the mean-times must be allowed to cut across this fundamental relationship. This is an order of creation: to see to it in the meantime, any meantime. Grief over a lost estate of prosperity must not filter down to soak the children with senseless tears. Loss of domain must not creep into the house of a daughter and suck her under grief, too. Despair at being unable to move or pay or deny or beg or acquire or restore must not throttle down to emptiness the thrust and zeal and power of fellowship. Let no one impose his own meantime on younger hearts and weaker backs. Let him carry his meantime out of sight.

I have seen with my own eyes the violation of this principle from Jeremiah's letter destroy the witness of a virile Christian home, wreck the health of a daughter, alienate a husband, distort two wonderful boys, and put an ailing mother-in-law in an institution in less than two years. There is a fellowship—even of exile—even of suffering—that must not be distorted in the meantime.

There is a future to be prepared for: "Give your daughters in marriage, that they may bear sons and daughters; multiply there, and do not decrease."

People are always leaving the theater before the show is over. They never see the end of the play; nor hear the benediction. Sometimes even the actors throw up their hands and leave before the curtain falls. Thus did Judas —and thus do men today. Jeremiah is saying that there is a difference between the end of things and the edge of things. He will say it again and again. There is a future from anywhere a person stands. He must quit marking off his own potential. He must not despair of anybody or anything until God gets through. As Chicken Little ran from an acorn, so man runs from life's normal meantimes as if any acorn, or any meantime could be an *end* of anything. There is a future from wherever he is, even when he can see the lights of the city.

And in the meantime—now comes Jeremiah's most shocking and heretical statement to these Jerusalem-loving Jews, heartsick for their native streets and haunts. It is heresy; it is treason; but while they are kept from their Jerusalem, says the Lord: "Seek the welfare of the city where I have sent you into exile, and pray to the Lord on its behalf."

This is hard to take. Loving Jerusalem, aching to return, held captive in Babylon, they are to learn to love the scene of their captivity—Babylon—and to pray for their place of exile—to seek the peace of the city where they are captive. And *pray* for it.

That is to say, with Alfred Whitehead, "It is a mistake to cling to a region through which one has already passed." Man must put down some roots where he is. There is a need in Babylon, he must seek the peace of the city where he is.

There is no escape from the captivity of a meantime that will not seek the peace of the city where it lies captive. Dostoevsky's friends kept a Christmas in Siberia; and the wreckage of men held at Andersonville tried to build houses out of stumps, and the Count of Monte Cristo, in his cell, had a vine and a flower to watch. They put down some roots in their meantime. This is the key to Jeremiah's letter. Without this one has no hope. The individual inhabits his own meantime in sheer loneliness and boredom like to that of hell. He waves the petty flags of his belligerent allegiance to a former estate; he advertises his dissatisfactions with any job, any house, any hymn, any teacher, any work, any sermon—because he has no roots and must display his color swiftly, for he is rootless and cannot live—long—in the meantime.

This was hard for Jews in Babylon's muddy flats. This is hard teaching for those in a culture that changes its people and its center faster than they can move from one apartment shopping center to its mate. But there's a healing in it.

Jeremiah's letter tells the Jews to do the next thing, there's a healing in it; to remember the fellowship around them and not impose their agonies on younger backs; and to put down some roots where they are. He urges them to seek the peace of the city and pray for it.

There's a healing in this.

What if the only peace a person gets is Babylon's kind of peace? What if the years of his captivity swept over him and washed him away until he had no chance for peace except the peace he could have had in the Babylon where he is? What if that he now has with his own in this place is all he gets?

The Lord through Jeremiah says the Jews had better take their peace now: "for in its welfare [of Babylon, that is] you will find your welfare."

They have a return on their investment, he says. The welfare of Babylon *is* their welfare, the only welfare they get, where they are. Their recovery from meantime rests on their making Babylon peaceful. Babylon is home, and in Babylon's welfare is the welfare of all.

Refuse the false daydreaming prophets, Jeremiah tells them, God has not sent them or the words about Utopia. Life has its fill of Babylonian meantimes—and Babylon's welfare is the welfare of those who dwell there.

Do this, he says, for this is the end and defeat of meantime living. For God will come, even to Babylon: "For thus says the LORD: when seventy years are completed for Babylon, I will visit you, and I will fulfill to you my promise and bring you back to this place. For I know the plans I have for you, says the LORD, plans for welfare and not for evil, to give you a future and a hope."

Meantime is, in the last analysis, to be lived through for its own sake in the light of God's purpose for it and for his people: he tells them to do the next thing regarding fellow sufferers, in consciousness that there is an *edge* and a future. Today as then man must take cognizance of the need where he is, put down his roots, seeking the peace of the city as his own peace; this is the return on his investment: there is an end to his waiting, there is Someone to hear and to find. Indeed there is One whom to seek *is* to find: "After the seventy years," he says, "I will come to see you," the Lord himself will inhabit man's captivity, and will send man's word—speak man's word—write man's word—none of these—

God will do his good word—in that to which he returns his people.

The paradox of the history of Israel opens here. In all captivities God is at work—*doing* (historizing) his word. All the promises to Israel flower here: The Lord God invades, intrudes, breaks through to man's infirmities, *in* man's meantimes—and then? "Then you will call upon me and come and pray to me, and I will hear you. You will seek me and find me; when you seek me with all your heart."

Mendelssohn, the Jew, understands this paradox and wrests that phrase from all its local contexts, as Stanley Romaine Hopper says, and flings it with "unforgettable and uncannily haunting melody" into the midst of Elijah's lostness after Carmel:

> "If with all your heart ye truly seek me,
> Ye shall ever surely find me—"

And the meantime paradox is that Elijah and Jeremiah had already been found—in their own meantimes.

And Pascal in *Pensees* said: "Console yourself, thou wouldst not be seeking me hadst thou not already found me."

Is the finding in the seeking? Or is it that as man seeks him, he discovers He has found *him?*

Biographical Sketch

CHARLES L. ALLEN

There are not many preachers who make such an impact on a community that it attracts the attention of a secular journal like *Time* magazine. Yet, when Charles L. Allen was serving a Methodist Church in Atlanta, his influence was so widespread that *Time* did a feature story on him. At the time he was preaching to overflow crowds both in the morning and in the evening, and was reaching thousands more by a regular column that appeared in the local paper. Such a ministry not only attracted the attention of journalists but of many people, both in the church and out, who sought his counsel, guidance, and help. Interestingly enough, he did it without any sensationalism, any flares of oratory or any unusual gimmick, but, as the *Time*[1] article pointed out, simply by talking to people about the Christian life.

At present he is the pastor of the First Methodist Church in Houston, one of the largest Protestant congregations in the country. His preaching has extended far beyond his local congregation by means of lectures, preaching missions, radio, television and his books.

His books, primarily of an inspirational nature, have sold more than half a million copies. Some of them are: *God's Psychiatry, All Things Are Possible Through Prayer, When You Lose a Loved One, In Quest of God's Power, The Touch of the Master's Hand, Christmas in Our Hearts*.

Here, in his own words, he gives a background of his purpose and philosophy of preaching which, in his case, must meet the demands of a downtown church in a large urban area.

> For the past fifteen years it has been my assignment to preach in what we call "downtown" churches. My congregations have been made up of three groups of people: (1) a few who continue to live close in, (2) visitors from hotels and motels, (3) those who live in the suburbs. By far the largest part of the attendance is from that third group.

[1] Nov. 12, 1951.

That brings up the question of why a person will drive eight or ten miles, past several other churches, and come downtown. There are a number of answers to that question but the main answer is they come to hear a particular preacher. And the successful preacher in the downtown church must speak to the needs of individual people. Some people attend church out of loyalty or a sense of duty, others for social fellowship or for various other reasons, but usually they go to a church some distance away because they receive help from that particular minister and church.

In order to help the person, the minister must somehow get it across that he does love the people in his pews and that his purpose is to help and not hurt. A well-meaning person said to a minister friend of mine, "You ought to preach to people about their sins more and tell them what guilty sinners they are." My friend replied, "Do you recall how many Jesus saved by telling them they were sinners?"

Actually the minister should preach about sin and he should seek to bring about conviction of sin on the part of his people. But the way he does it is what is important. I knew of a Methodist church which went to the Bishop at the end of the year and demanded that he move their preacher. The reason they gave was that he was always preaching on hell. The Bishop did move the preacher but sent them another one who also regularly preached on hell. He was surprised the next year when the same people asked that their pastor be returned for another year.

The Bishop said, "Last year you wanted your preacher moved because he preached about hell. This year you want your minister returned, yet I know he preaches on hell as often as the other one. What is the difference?"

"The difference is this," they replied, "the first one told us we were going to hell and he seemed glad of it. The second one tells us we are going to hell and it seems to break his heart."

In my own preaching I have sought to deal with the sins of people and have sought to hold up solutions and hope. One of the deep problems of most people is a sense of guilt. We have done things we should not have done and left undone things we should have done. This is not only a source of worry but can lead to a deep sickness.

The human mind is like the body in that it can be wounded. If a person cuts his finger, it may not hurt much but, if he is not careful, this cut can become infected and the infection can spread over his body and may even be fatal. The mind also can be wounded. Sorrow is a wound. It cuts deeply and hurts terribly but sorrow is a clean wound. Unless bitterness, resentment, self-pity, or some other poison, gets into the wound of sorrow, it will heal.

Sin is also a wound but it is an unclean wound. When a person does wrong, his misdeed wounds his mind. The wound does not heal but it grows, it goes over his nervous system and makes him jittery; it goes to his stomach and upsets his digestion; it goes to his heart and accelerates its action; it goes to his backbone and takes the steel out of it. Nothing makes a man a coward more quickly than a sense of guilt.

The accompanying sermon is one which I have preached in an effort to help those with a burden of guilt. I am quite aware that this one sermon does not cover the entire problem. One great advantage of preaching in the same pulpit each Sunday is that the preacher does not feel he has to say everything in one sermon. He said some things last Sunday and he will have a chance to say more next Sunday.

This sermon was preached as one of a series to help those with a sense of guilt.

Six Facts About Forgiveness

"Forgive us our debts."—Matthew 6:12

IN THE LORD'S PRAYER we pray "Forgive us our debts." Instead of saying "debts," many use the word "transgressions" or "sins," but the word "debt" has vivid meaning for most of us. Debts can be a terrible burden. To know that all our debts are paid in full is a glorious experience.

In college I had to borrow some money to help pay the expenses, so when I started preaching, I was in debt. I was required to make a payment on what I owed each month. I had an old car but it finally wore completely out and I traded for a new one. I signed a contract to pay a certain amount a month until it was paid for. Paying for that car is where I got my best idea of eternity.

I remember some of the letters the finance company wrote when I got behind on my car payments. They were fearful. Once when I got two months behind, the man came after the car. I never talked so fast in my life. If I could preach as good as I talked to that man, I would make a lot of converts.

In those years we didn't have many clothes but we had to buy some as we went along. It was illegal to go without clothes. What we bought were always purchased on the installment plan. I remember an overcoat I bought for $5 down and $5 a month. I missed so many payments that by the time I finally made the last one, the coat was threadbare. We bought even our groceries on credit. Because my credit at the grocery store was so limited is one reason I am so skinny today.

In those years it took every dollar I got to pay for something I had already eaten up or worn out. It worried me to be in debt. I don't remember asking God to let those debts be "forgiven," but I did pray many times asking God to show me how to make enough money to pay up everything.

One thing I did to get extra money was referee basketball games. I was paid $5 a game and I never worked so hard at anything else and took so much cussing for so little. I remember the last game I refereed. It was a girls' game and that was the worst kind. After the game a little girl told me, "You may be a preacher but you are going straight to hell." I decided she may be right.

I worked hard, the Lord helped me and finally there came the day when all my debts were paid. I didn't owe any more payments, there were no more mean letters about being behind, what money I had was clear and free. A great burden was lifted from my mind and I felt new joy and happiness.

But debts for cars and clothes and other things are not the worst ones. There is the burden of debt that comes because of our sins against God. How can we ever feel that debt is paid?

Most of us know the burden of being in debt. I used to trade with a grocer who kept his accounts in a big book. I would pay him as I could and he would mark "paid" by certain items but the trouble was I had to keep on eating, so I would charge other things. It was hard to ever get the page completely paid off.

As children we got the idea that God kept a list of our sins in a big book. Each of those sins was like a debt we owed and would have to pay. Some of our sins we felt we could pay for by doing something real good. Sometimes when trouble or misfortune came, we felt God was making us pay in that way. But we never could catch up because we would do other things that were bad and they would be recorded against us.

Finally we get to the place that we feel that we can never pay off our debt of sin to God. We feel hopelessly doomed. Then it is we remember that Jesus taught us to pray, "Forgive us our debts" (Matthew 6:12). Will God answer that prayer? Can we know that the page against us in God's book is marked "paid in full"? Can we really feel forgiven? We can if we will accept six facts—not just in our minds but also in our hearts:

(1) God wants to forgive us. He loves us and understands us. The Bible tells us, "If we confess our sins, he is faithful and just, and will forgive our sins" (1 John 1:9). Why should we confess? God already knows all about us. Confession is our recognition that what we have done is wrong, it also means our desire to have it taken out of our lives and hearts. We do not need to persuade God to forgive. As we look at the cross, we realize that he loves us and goes to the uttermost for us.

(2) Forgiveness means that we are again on good terms with God. It does not take away the memory of our wrongs. We shall never forget them. The pain and sorrow of our failures will always remain with us. Neither does forgiveness take away all the consequences of our sins. Some of our sins we will pay for until we die. But forgiveness does mean that a right relationship with God is restored. We can again respond to his love. His power and peace can flow freely into our hearts. We do not feel cut off and alone. We feel in our hearts that he is our Father and we are his children.

(3) God does not expect us to rid ourselves of our sins. The old song has it right: "Just as I am—I come, I come." God is not some tyrant who takes delight in making us feel condemned and who wants to whip us. I once had a schoolteacher who seemed to get real joy out of using a big leather strap he had. I was so afraid of him

I never learned much in his class. God is not like that. He says, "I know what is troubling you. I don't expect you to conquer all the evil thoughts and desires in your heart. But come and let me help you and together we will find the right way. I will walk with you to guide and strengthen and help you find joy and satisfaction."

(4) When we have been forgiven, we can go on. God expects that. He doesn't want us to keep on confessing the same sin. He doesn't want us to keep chewing over the past. When Jesus says God is a father, he helps me because I had an earthly father who was like what I want to believe God is like. One of Papa's rules with his children was to settle whatever wrong we had done before we went to bed. If we needed talking to, he never put it off until tomorrow. After it was settled, he never mentioned it again, nor would he permit us to.

God is a Father who settles things. Forgiveness means we have been set free to go on living and we are expected to go on. To face it, settle it, go on is the way to deal with sin before God.

(5) Forgiveness means that we surrender that wrong and that we surrender to God. Why do we do something that is wrong? Because we can't help it? No, because we don't want to help it. We do wrong things because we enjoy them, or because we profit by them. As long as the joy we receive from wrong is greater than the joy of a right relationship with God, we shall keep on. But when we decide, truly decide, that we want God more than that wrong, then are we willing to give it up.

Also, we cannot say to God, "I am yours but on my terms." Again and again have I talked with someone in regard to making his life right with God. Often he has said, "But I am not sure about what God wants me to do." My reply is, "Completely decide that you will do the right thing. Then when you have committed yourself, God will show you what the right thing is." God gives insight to those who trust him.

(6) If we do not feel forgiven, it is likely because of our own pride. It is easy to tell ourselves, "I'm not such a bad fellow. I really don't need any help." We think of many good things we have done. We list the better qualities of our lives. Then we remind ourselves of the mean things other people do that we haven't done. We decide we can get along without God's forgiveness. Yet such talk is only pretending. We know that we are guilty, that we cannot save ourselves. It takes a strong man to get on his knees before God.

In *Pilgrim's Progress*, Christian was making his way toward the Eternal City. On his back was the burden of his sins. He came to Calvary, climbed to the top, and knelt at the cross. His sins were loosed; they rolled down the hill into a sepulcher and were buried forever. Then Christian said with a merry heart, "He has given me rest by his sorrow and life by his death."

Forgiveness is a miracle which God performs. I do not explain it. I simply say: "In my hand no price I bring; simply to thy cross I cling."

Biographical Sketch

Edwin L. Becker lived the first twenty-one years of his life in the predominantly agricultural state of Iowa. The son of a minister, he graduated from Drake University. His seminary studies were at Yale University Divinity School where he also received the Ph.D. degree. His interests in the rural church also took him to the University of Wisconsin for study in rural sociology and the M.A. degree.

For two years he was pastor of the Christian churches in the Brock-Peru Pastoral Unity in Nebraska. Then, for six years he served as National Director of Town and Country work for his denomination, Disciples of Christ. Returning to Yale for graduate study, he was Lecturer in the Rural Church and Supervisor of Religious Field Work. Since 1953 he has been at the Divinity School of Drake University where he is Professor of Applied Christianity and Director of Religious Field Work.

In the summer of 1953 he traveled and studied in Europe and was a member of an International Conference on the Church in Rural Life held at the Ecumenical Institute, Bossey, Switzerland. During the year 1961-62 he was again abroad, studying and lecturing for nine months at William Temple College, Rugby, England, and for two months visiting centers of religious research and church renewal on the Continent. He is presently chairman of the Fellowship of Professors of Town and Country Church.

Dr. Becker describes the background for this sermon as follows:

> The measure of good preaching is the degree to which it brings the reality of God to people within the context of their daily life. It is my belief that the sermon is not so much in itself the confrontation with the word of God as it is the instrument by which the hearers are encouraged and enabled to recognize and respond to the living God in the concerns and work of each day. God's word is not afar off, to be brought by the preacher from heaven. It is near at hand, in the very midst of life. God is to be known decisively

not in some acts designated as "religious experiences," but in events related to the most real concerns of people. He becomes known to those who have eyes to see and ears to understand that his demanding and redeeming word is present in every situation. The pulpit must endeavor to point men to God by way of their most meaningful experiences throughout life.

Today the rural minister senses that people have difficulty in relating the reality of God to the realities of their daily existence. This is in part because God has become a symbol of something that is in the past. He is identified with a preindustrial society. He is not sensed as a present living reality which men must take into account except in certain largely personal experiences in the family and close neighborhood relationships. God seems strange to mechanized agriculture and remote from the changes in community life which disturb rural people. It is to this situation that the sermon here is directed. The aim, however poorly realized, has been to open to this rural congregation, predominantly agricultural, the realization that the same God who worked with his people in the period of the Exodus still works with us today through the world to which we must give ourselves.

An
Exceedingly Good Land

*"The land, which we passed through to spy it out,
is an exceedingly good land."*—Numbers 14:7

THERE IS AN ANCIENT STORY of a nomadic tribe of people
which one day stood at the border of a new and strange
land. Out of timidity and prudence they sent certain
trusted leaders across the border to spy out the new land
and bring reports. For forty days these appointed men
tramped about in the wilderness. From behind trees and
rocks they looked at the people. In the darkness of night
they walked about the cities. They found rich fruits and
nuts in the fields which they picked and ate. The cities
were strongly walled, the people they saw were healthy
and well fed, their tools and implements were queer. The
spies, their minds filled with strange visions and stirred
by their experiences in this new land, returned to make
their report.

Like the parable of the blind men describing the ele-
phant, these twelve, although they had traveled in the
same land, held widely differing views of what they had
seen. One said, "It flows with milk and honey, and this
is its fruit." And he held before the people great clusters
of large grapes. "Let us go up at once and occupy it,"
he said, "for we are well able to overcome it." But several
of his companions were of quite a different point of view.
"We are not able to go up against the people, for they
are stronger than we. It is a land that devours its inhabitants; and all the people that we saw in it are men
of great stature." In fact, said these spies, "There we saw
giants; and we seemed to ourselves like grasshoppers,
and so we seemed to them." Their report brought fear

to the hearts of the people. The people wept and longed for the security of their former home. They drew back and would not go into the new land, and they were led into a wilderness where they wandered aimlessly for forty years.

In many ways we are the people of that ancient story. We are, in the first place, like them, the people of God. These Hebrew people had been elected by God, gathered together and delivered from the bondage in Egypt, and summoned to be his people in the world. We, too, are that people. We who have once heard and heeded the call of God in Jesus Christ are bound together as his body, as his grateful servants. The writer of 1 Peter described our situation. "You are a chosen race, a royal priesthood, a holy nation, God's own people, that you may declare the wonderful deeds of him who called you out of darkness into his marvelous light. Once you were no people but now you are God's people; once you had not received mercy but now you have received mercy."

Most of us, when we hear those words today, look around at one another and ask, "Who, me?" "That surely cannot mean us, this group of friends and neighbors who meet peacefully here each Sunday morning." We are pretty well satisfied with things just as they are. We are not aware of any great need for more light. We certainly are not setting out on any crusade. In fact, if we are chosen for any great undertaking that might take us out of our comfortable homes or cause any sacrifices, we had better take another look at this church business.

The trouble is, however, that these words of the epistle of Peter do refer to us, the members of the church. We cannot so easily escape. We need to take another look at what it means to be God's own people in our day and generation, to sense again what it is that God through his gracious Son has done for us.

Those chosen people at the border of Canaan did not wear their yoke easily. They were a restless and rebellious folk. God had to forgive them again and again. They were given a new chance time after time. But underlying their life together was the sense that they did belong to God. Always they were called back again to be his people, his servants in the world. So it is with us in this day.

We are this people, in the second place, because we too stand on the borders of a new and strange land. We who dwell in a rural community in America stand as the first mature generation within a culture and a way of life as different from the land of our fathers as Canaan was different from the wilderness of Sinai. Many of us in this congregation grew up with kerosene lamps and the wood stove. We went to town once a week and our children were fortunate if they completed eight grades in school. As far as we were concerned in our youth, the gasoline engine and the wireless had not been invented. Horses and men's backs supplied the power for our work and the little time we were not working was spent with close neighbors. In that life God was remembered not only on Sunday in church but daily at family prayers.

Today, like the children of Israel, we stand on the threshold of a culture, a civilization which is both terrifying and appealing to us in its power and affluence. No matter how we may feel about it, this new society will not go away nor can we turn away from it. This is God's gift to his people and we are called to go into it and possess it, not for ourselves but for him.

The reports from our spies are just as conflicting as were those who reported to that band on the borders of Canaan. This new land in which we live bears fruit in unbelievable abundance. It is a land flowing in milk and honey. The average yield we take for granted today was not dreamed of a generation ago. In this harvest season, with corn piled high on the ground and cribs literally bulging with the yield, can anyone doubt that this is a good land, a blessed land, through which God is sustaining physical life in abundance? The farmer's production today feeds and clothes not only himself but more than twenty-five other persons as well.

There are, however, other reports less favorable than these coming from this strange land. There are those who can also say that it is a land of giants, that it devours its inhabitants. There are many who in the midst of the monumental changes which surround them feel themselves like grasshoppers. There are machines in this new land which can devour us. When men working long hours are weary and careless, these giants have claimed limbs and even life itself.

In other ways do the forces at work in this new culture devour the inhabitants. They have forced the enlargement of farms if men are to be fully employed and if income is to be adequate. Many of our neighbors have been forced to leave their farms. In this state (Iowa) more than one out of ten farms has been consolidated. Our economists predict that there will be still twenty-five percent fewer farms in another ten years. With fewer people, businesses must often close and all the institutions of our community suffer loss of leaders. Our own sons and daughters must look to other communities, usually the cities, for their future life. These economic forces seem to drive us to greater and greater effort, to larger and larger farms, to heavier and heavier indebtedness, to frightening investments.

Here we are, situated within a new and in many ways baffling society. What are we to do with it? More important, we must ask, what are we to do with ourselves?

Like the Hebrews on the borders of Canaan, we can grumble and complain. We can remember the good old days. We can waste our energies wishing for a return to a day which God has forever taken away from us.

Or we can make our peace with it and say this is a pretty good world and we might just as well get the most out of it. That is what most of us have said. We will eat and drink and be merry for tomorrow it will be somebody else's problem. The rhyme of the five little pigs has to be rewritten for our day. Now, all the little pigs have roast beef, none of them stay home, and all are crying "we," "we," "we." The results of this way of facing the world of material abundance will be for us and for all men a life in the wilderness. We will have forgotten whence we have come and we will have no idea where we are going. All purpose and meaning is lost. This is the answer of the successful farmer in Jesus' parable. His land produced abundantly. He had so much that he had to ask, "What shall I do, for I have no place to store my crops?" He built new and larger barns and, when he had his crop safely stored, he actually believed that nothing else now mattered. "But God said to him, 'Fool! This night your soul is required of you; and the things you have prepared, whose will they be?" And Jesus concludes his story, "So is he who lays up treasure for himself, and is not rich toward God."

There is still a third way open to us. We need not stand wringing our hands, longing for a return to days that are gone. Neither are we to take the way of a sensate and meaningless materialism. If we can grasp again the reality that we are fundamentally God's people, we can yet possess this land and use the abundance that is ours in the service of his kingdom.

To know that we are the people of God will bring again into the center of life the sense that God is leading this world. In order to find themselves again, men must find life centering in the living God.

> "It is he that made us, and we are his;
> we are his people, and the sheep of his pasture.
> —Psalm 100:3

This world with all of its economic power, its giant machines, its costly technology and industry, is still God's world. It is sustained by his creative power. We who are God's people should know this and witness to it before both the nostalgic ones and those who have found it easier to act as though God is dead. We must say that God is; that the new world is his no less than the world of another day.

We will, furthermore, as God's people, sense that we are to serve his redemptive purposes. As men are drawn to God they are brought into a relationship of love and concern for one another. Our material abundance will become an instrument for God's purpose for our brethren whom we cannot see. Christian stewardship will become the guiding economic principle in our lives. We become aware that the good life does not consist in the abundance of the things which are seen. Our standard of living becomes less important than the standard of our lives.

God's people are to live both joyfully and obediently. Like the people of that ancient story, we may often be slow to trust God and we may often want our way more than we want to follow his. But soon and late God prevails and the prophetic word becomes reality. "The land . . . is an exceedingly good land. If the LORD delights in us, he will bring us into this land and give it to us, a land which flows with milk and honey. Only, do not rebel against the LORD." Nor let us forget who we are, for we are God's own people. Let us go in to claim this new land for him.

Biographical Sketch

J. WALLACE HAMILTON

J. Wallace Hamilton has served more than thirty years as the pastor of the Pasadena Community Church, St. Petersburg, Florida. His ministry has been most unusual. When he assumed the pastorate of the church as a young man of thirty, it was in a run-down condition with a dwindling attendance. Many predicted it would have to close completely before long. Soon, however, the church was not only filled with people who wanted to hear Dr. Hamilton preach, but the sanctuary had to be enlarged. When the enlarged sanctuary was filled every Sunday, people began sitting on benches outside. Then someone conceived the idea of using the cars parked outside the church to care for the overflow. Loudspeakers were installed for this purpose. Soon additional parking lots and better speaking equipment had to be added. Now, on any given Sunday, more people may hear his sermon outside than in. While 2,000 can be accommodated in the church, as many may be seated outside on benches, and as many more in cars. More than sixty lay ushers are required to direct the parking of the cars.

Dr. Hamilton has preached and lectured from coast to coast, including the Chicago Sunday Evening Club and Riverside Church in New York City. He has delivered the Quillian Lectures at Emory University and the John M. English Lectures at Andover Newton Theological School. The content and nature of his preaching may be found in three volumes of sermons: *Horns and Halos, Ride the Wild Horses,* and *Who Goes There?*

In one of these sermons, entitled "The Image of God,"[1] he uses an illustration from the life of John Wesley. "John Wesley records in his journal that one day, preaching to the miners, he used the text, 'But as many as received him, to them gave he power to become the sons of God. . . .' Then he added a characteristic note: 'They seemed greatly encouraged.'" One might add that many people who live in and around St. Petersburg have been encouraged by Dr. Hamilton's preaching as well.

---

[1] In *Who Goes There?* (Westwood, N. J.: Fleming H. Revell Co., 1958), p. 82.

Dr. Hamilton says: "Once a year I attempt to preach on the healing power of Christian faith with a recognition of deepening understanding between ministers in the cure of souls and psychotherapists in their commendable concern about bringing order into disordered life. The following sermon is one of such attempts."

Overcoming
Emotional Depression

"Out of the depths I cry to thee, O LORD!"
—Psalm 130:1

I WONDER IF THE PSALMIST knew what was wrong with him. I wonder if millions today, in the depths of emotional depression, know what is really wrong with them.

In recent years there has been much good-natured discussion about what constitutes a normal person. Who is normal? What do we mean when we say of someone, "He is a normal human being"? It is a bit like asking what is a nice day. Ask a dozen people, "What is a nice day?" and you will get a dozen different answers. That word "normal" is a word with considerable elasticity in it. It doesn't mean perfection; if it did, no one would be normal. And it doesn't mean average. I am five feet six; a young friend of mine here is six feet four. Neither of us is average, but we are both normal. There are reasonable variations between people normal in height, weight, mental capacity, and so on.

When we come into the delicate area of temperament and emotional behavior, that is still true. There is no sharp, clear-cut distinction between normal and abnormal. We are all neurotic to some extent; that is, we all have nerves. We have emotions, and they sometimes misbehave abnormally. We all have our ups and downs, our good days and bad days. Everybody gets depressed at times.

What we are getting at in this sermon is that shadowy borderland between normal and abnormal, that fuzzy halfway place where normal people have trouble with their emotions and occasionally go down into the depths to get a temporary taste of what emotionally sick people experience chronically.

Picture an imaginary line running horizontally through life—below it darkness, above it light. William James called it "the threshold"—the misery threshold, the symbolic point of mood where one state of mind passes over into another. Above that line we control our emotions. We may have ups and downs in it but we are master of our moods. When we dip below it, we are in trouble. We don't control our emotions. They control us. We are at the mercy of our moods. That misery line varies in different people just as the pain line varies. Some people can stand an enormous amount of pain. In others the pain threshold is high. But in all of us there is a line somewhere below which we are at the mercy of our moods.

It seems that the more sensitive we are, the more susceptible we are. It would be interesting if we had time here to go back through history and call the roll of the great who shared the psalmist's experience: Beethoven, Tschaikowsky, Tolstoy, Samuel Johnson, Abraham Lincoln—gifted, sensitive, conscientious people.

It would be interesting, too, to consider the various names by which the experience has been known. Bunyan called it "the slough of despond." St. John at the Cross called it "the dark night of the soul." The army calls it "operational fatigue." The psychiatrist calls it "anxiety neurosis." The layman calls it "nervous exhaustion." The psalmist, not knowing the names, simply said, "Out of the depths I cry to thee."

How does it happen? Bodily sickness can produce it. We are body minds—part chemical, part spiritual—and what affects the one influences the other. A depleted physical vitality can be the open door to emotional disorder. Any chemical deficiency, whether through malnutrition, anemia, or glandular imbalance, may be the

beginning of an emotional tailspin. Low spirits are often
the result of low physical vitality.

Tensions may produce it. Dr. Richard Hoffman of
New York says that civilization's three major killers are
not heart disease, cancer, and accidents, but calendars,
telephones, and clocks—the tyranny of an accelerated life.
When an office building in Detroit has been nicknamed
"Ulcer Alley," it means that more is breaking in on the
nervous system today than it was fashioned to cope with.
Men drive themselves beyond their power to endure. The
price of financial success is mounting higher. The com-
petitive struggle is cruel and ruthless. Millions are living
in subconscious fear. They worry about their jobs, their
health, about getting old, and about the security of their
dependents. And the more they worry about their problems, the more they unfit themselves to handle them, and
the closer to that threshold line they come. Many a solid
citizen today, caught in modern tensions, has dipped below the line, wondering what in the world is the matter
with him. He feels he has lost his grip. He has spells of
weakness. A sense of foreboding dread hangs over him.
A vague uneasiness is in him. He wonders if he's losing
his mind, or maybe he is going to die. He has simply
dipped below the line into the depths where emotions,
meant to be the driving force of life, have become the
destroying force.

Sometimes ethical conflict produces it—indecision between what we want to do and what we know we ought
to do. A noted physician said a good percentage of people coming to the doctor's office do not need medicine
half as much as a good dose of old-fashioned conversion;
by which he meant, of course, that when the sickness is
moral, there is no use trying to cure it with pills.

We are people who have inherited from our fathers a
vital religion. We were brought up in homes where we
were taught certain ethical ideals about marriage and

divorce, about the use of intoxicants, and so on. But by and large, we have not been living up to these ideals. Our generation has swung far away from them, called them "old-fashioned," has boasted loudly of modern freedom; only to find that conscience is not so easily dismissed, that right and wrong are not something in a book but something written in our natures, that the unconscious mind is more old-fashioned than our freedom. The sense of guilt is making people sick. Whether it is remorse over real or imaginary sins, the result is the same. The weight of unforgiven sin hangs heavily over many.

Now we have sketched briefly and inadequately some of the causative factors. There are many others—hereditary influences, shock, prolonged bereavement; many factors and combination of factors get people down in the depths.

How do they get up? I am quite aware that some people reading this will have only a vague idea what we are talking about. They will wonder why a minister would take up a whole service on a subject so remote from life. I am also sure that others will be eagerly listening, for they are praying right now the psalmist's prayer: "Out of the depths do I cry." And still others, if not below the line, are living perilously close to it, day by day trying desperately not to go to pieces.

I want to put down a few simple, practical rules. *First:* Never accept any present mood as permanent. It usually comes as a great relief to one who is down in the depths when it begins to dawn on him that what has happened to him is a rather common ailment shared by many others, that it is not unusual, not fatal, and not permanent. It takes some of the unknown terror out of the darkness to be assured that he is not losing his religion as he thinks, or his soul, or his mind. Part of the cure is in understanding what has really happened to him, why he feels so utterly unlike himself. He will begin to discount his morbid, depressed feelings when he understands they are caused by emotional misbehavior and not by any of the gloomy things he is thrashing around in his mind. There's no use telling him to snap out of it, for that is exactly what he can't do. It's a cruel thing to tell him there is nothing wrong with him, that it's all in his mind, because while it is in his mind, it is deeper than his reason in his feeling. Feelings are always more powerful than thoughts.

Fortunately, in some respects, our moods are like the weather—changeable. Up in New England they have an expression: "If you don't like our weather, wait a minute." And that is the first thing to do—wait, and realize that while right now you are under a cloud, yet behind the cloud the sun still shines. And one day the cloud will pass and you will be out in the clear again. Never accept the present mood as permanent.

Second: Tell it to somebody. "What the average woman wants," goes an old saying, "is not a doctor but an audience." We all need an audience at times. Tell it out to somebody, not everybody lest you make yourself a nuisance, and not just anybody. Find some wholesome, skilled person if you can, who will provide a listening and understanding ear. Get all the trouble up and out. We had a popular song back in World War I: "Pack up your troubles in your old kit bag and smile," which is about the very worst thing anyone can do with troubles. You can't get rid of your troubles by packing them down in the kit bag of your unconscious self, or by bottling them up inside behind a determined grin. Hold them up in the open where you can look at them, ventilate them in the presence of some wholesome person who may, especially if he has some understanding of the nature of the emotional illness, be able to interpret for you, or better help you to interpret for yourself, the unpleasant stimuli back of your distress.

People who are having trouble with their emotions could, in many cases, do much to help themselves keep out of the darkness by educating themselves about the nature of anxiety and fear—what fear is for and what it is not for. Fear is an emotion of "extremely high voltage." An anxiety attack can throw a person into as great a state of panic as though he were held up at the point of a gun. Fear can cause illness, speed up your heart, make it behave as though you had a heart attack. Fear can create illusions and obsessions and thought theories about yourself to stimulate the symptoms of almost any illness. You can fix in your mind feelings about yourself, your health, your husband, your relationship to God, which sometimes require months to dig up out of that old kit bag and air it in the light. It's a great help to have someone to whom you can air your troubles.

Three: Work out for yourself some tension-reducing device. If your descent into the depths has been caused by anxieties or faulty thinking about yourself, then obviously the way up is through straight thinking, relaxation from high tensions. If the problem has been induced by wrong emotional habits, the cure must lie in the development of right habits. That won't happen in a moment. There are no sudden miracles in the process. If you have been a worrier, tying yourself in nervous knots for thirty years, don't expect to untie the knots in thirty minutes. There are no ecclesiastical pliers with which you can reach in and untangle the crossed wires. All habits, good or bad, are formed by patient practice.

Here is a little device which many people have found helpful, and I am happy to pass it on. When you lie down at night and those thousand and one problems of the day begin to thrash through your mind, picture them as unwelcomed visitors to your home. Just outside your front door there is a walkway to the street and at the end of the walk, a gate. When one of these unpleasant visitors turns in from the street to disturb you, just go down the walk and shut the gate. Picture yourself doing that—down the walk and shut the gate. Practice that a while with your anxieties, your fears and tensions, quietly shut them out. Sleep is the relaxation of four hundred muscles.

Four: Link your emotions with affirmative thoughts about the power and greatness and goodness of God. If you're going to rest back, you need to have something to rest back upon. A moment ago we quoted William James. He is still generally known as the pioneer of American psychologists. What is not so generally known is that at twenty-eight, he suffered an almost complete breakdown in health. Torn with doubts, afraid of life, obsessed with the horror of ending up in an asylum, he dreaded to be left alone. "I was seized," he said, "with a despondency so deep that if I had not turned to Scripture texts such as, 'The eternal God is my refuge,' 'I am the resurrection and the life,' and so on, I think I should really have lost my mind."

It is not enough to relax. You need to relax your soul in God, rest back upon the everlasting arms, go down the walk and shut the gate, and say, "Here, Lord, will you please handle these visitors until I get strong enough to handle them?" A ton of care will drop from your shoulders when you let yourself go in God. Link your emotions with affirmative thoughts about his power and his goodness, and his forgiveness.

Five: Set yourself some reasonable program of action. There is a definite connection between the head, the heart, and the hand. The hand is the best instrument ever devised to get your attention off yourself. Some people never manage that. They turn their thoughts inward upon themselves. They are forever feeling their pulse, analyzing every nervous twitch. They are like the man driving his automobile with his eyes fixed on the panel board, so intent on the speedometer and oil gauge that he slides off the road into the ditch.

The hand is important. Develop some occupational interest to get your mind off yourself. Make it easy at first. Don't try to do too many things or finish anything too quickly. Don't challenge yourself with too great a load.

A famous American author got into the depths one time, and the harder he tried to come up, the deeper he went down. His first book was a best seller, and on the strength of that his publisher made a contract for a second and made a substantial down payment on it. Halfway through it, the author was stuck, petrified, unable to write a word; days and nights filled with horrible thoughts of failure, bankruptcy, futility. His wife helped him up—she got him up every morning as usual, set him down before his typewriter, not to write his book—he must forget that completely—but just to write whatever came into his head whether it made sense or not. Little by little, with all that load off him, in a kind of vocational freewheeling, he was back in stride; and in a few months was pounding out his book. Sometimes you have to back up, get the big load off your mind. What else did Jesus mean when he said, "Be not anxious about tomorrow. . . . Let the day's own trouble be sufficient for the day." Get tomorrow off your back.

> Life is hard, by the yard,
> But by the inch, it's a cinch.

Set for yourself some reasonable program of action.

Six: Help somebody else. There is no better medicine in the world than the stimulating tonic of love. Forget what it means to those upon whom it is bestowed; think for a while of what it means to you when you bestow it. Love is a great healing emotion. It casts out fear. It cures and conquers evil. It opens up the channels through which God's healing spirit flows. The best way up is to help some other person up. Love is the key to wholesomeness and health.

Now on the surface it may seem that we have forgotten what we started out to talk about, namely—the healing power of Christ. But of course we've been speaking of nothing else. He is the Great Physician. We have been only restating in other words the great rules of spiritual wholeness which he so explicitly taught. Some years ago I read a most entertaining and helpful book written by a psychiatrist, James Tucker Fisher. He was indeed a pioneer in psychiatry, studied under Freud, and for half a century majored in this field of psychosomatic medicine.

Near the close of his book which he calls *A Few Buttons Missing*, Dr. Fisher makes this rather startling summary.

What was needed, I felt sure, was some new and enlightened recipe for living a sane and satisfying life—a recipe compounded from all the accumulated scientific knowledge acquired through study and research.

. . . I dreamed of writing a handbook that would be simple, practical, easy to understand and easy to follow. It would tell people how to live—what thoughts and attitudes and philosophies to cultivate and what pitfalls to avoid, in seeking mental health. I attended every symposium it was possible for me to attend, and I took notes on the wise words of my teachers and of my colleagues who were leaders in their field.

And then, quite by accident, I discovered that such a work had already been completed.

For a specific illustration, I believe the following to be true: If you were to take the sum total of all the authoritative articles ever written by the most qualified psychologists and psychiatrists on the subject of mental hygiene—if you were to combine them, and refine them, and cleave out the excess verbiage—if you were to take the whole of the meat and none of the parsley, and if you were to have these unadulterated bits of pure scientific knowledge concisely expressed by the most capable of living poets, you would have an awkward and incomplete summation of the Sermon on the Mount. And it would suffer immeasurably through comparison.

For nearly two thousand years the Christian world has been holding in its hand the complete answer to its restless and fruitless yearnings.[1]

[1]From *A Few Buttons Missing* by James T. Fisher and Lowell S. Hawley (Philadelphia: J. B. Lippincott Co.).

ROBERT E. GOODRICH, JR.

Robert E. Goodrich is pastor of the First Methodist Church, Dallas, Texas. The son of a well-known Methodist minister, he was educated at Centenary College and Birmingham-Southern College and Southern Methodist University. Before coming to Dallas he held pastorates in Port Arthur, Galena Park, Houston, and El Paso, all in Texas.

A popular preacher and speaker, Dr. Goodrich has preached and lectured before many church assemblies and conventions, in college chapels, and at the Texas Cowboy Camp Meetings. Three volumes of his sermons have been published. They are: *What's It All About? Reach for the Sky,* and *Lift Up Your Heart.*

He was a pioneer in radio and television programming. For years his regular Sunday services have been broadcast. He has also given weekly religious commentary on the news and for nine years conducted a weekly dramatic television program, *The Pastor Calls.* Also a filmed series, *The Pastor,* was distributed to more than 300 television stations by the Broadcasting and Film Commission of the National Council of Churches. He served as the preacher for the Methodist series of the Protestant Radio Hour carried by 408 stations in North America and to the Armed Forces overseas.

The sermon which follows is one of the sermons presented in that series.

In the introduction to one of the books of sermons mentioned above, William C. Martin speaks of Dr. Goodrich's congregation and his purposes of preaching. His sermons, Bishop Martin said, "were preached to a congregation which represents as widely varied backgrounds and interests as can be found in any typical downtown church. They were born of the effort to deal directly, and from the viewpoint of the Christian convictions, with questions that cannot be held at arm's length for academic consideration and with urgent individual and social problems about which people must make up their minds because they must make up their lives."

He speaks of some of the dangers of a psychological approach to preaching and the solution which Dr. Goodrich has found:

101

We are just now in a day when a vast amount of ridicule and scorn is being heaped upon preachers who are making use of the findings and techniques of modern psychology in an effort to give a greater degree of inner security to individual believers. Insofar as this kind of preaching becomes divorced from the basic Christian requirements of genuine repentance and true faith, it deserves this caustic rebuke. The Good News of God can never be equated with superficial panaceas for avoiding worry and achieving success; dependable faith and courage cannot be secured by a skillful manipulation of the emotions. In full recognition of this important truth, it must also be said that there is urgent need for the kind of preaching that seeks to enable sincere believers to enter into the full use and enjoyment of their inheritance.

Many people fail to reach the full stature of Christian living, not because they are lacking in a basic commitment to the demands of Christian truth, but because they have never been taught the simple and elemental practices and habits which can become the connecting channels between the boundless grace of God and the areas of human need. There can never be valid substitutes in Christian living for self-surrender and faith, but there will always be need, after these requirements have been met, for intelligent and historically tested disciplines by which the will of God becomes operative in individual and corporate life.[1]

---

[1] Robert E. Goodrich, Jr., *What's It All About?* (Westwood, N. J.: Fleming H. Revell Co., 1955). Introduction.

How to
Handle Your Load

EVERY FEW WEEKS somebody publishes a new analysis of television programs. It usually leads to a discouraging conclusion concerning the intellectual age of either the audience or the producers. The dilemma seems to be this: The audience says, "We've got to look at what they give us," and the producers say, "We've got to give them what they'll look at!" The cycle would appear to be hopeless, yet recently some fine new programs have been introduced.

An equally interesting analysis could be made of the commercials on television and radio from the standpoint of the products and services offered to the public. I have never seen a chart; but my impression is that, high up on the list, would be the category of medicine and treatments for nervous tension and headaches, along with other physical manifestations of strain, worry, and anxiety.

In other words, judging from what television and radio commercials offer, as well as in newspaper and magazine advertising, there must be an abundance of customers for these particular medicines. Evidently a large percentage of the people in the United States have need of some kind of help in handling the anxieties and tensions which result from the pressure or the "load" of life.

A clinic in New Orleans has made a study of the common headache. After the findings were presented to a medical society, they were summarized in the newspapers. It was discovered that 65 percent of the people regularly have headaches, more or less severe. (No wonder so many different kinds of headache remedies are advertised.) The study revealed also that single persons have more headaches than married people, but that widows and widowers have least of all. Most prone to headaches are the supermeticulous persons who have never learned to live in easy harmony with God and man. Another large category is made up of those who lead hurried, hectic lives of desperation. The burdens of life simply get them down.

Frankly, it is not the physical load we carry that breaks us and leaves us fatigued; it is the inner load of conflicts and fears and anxieties. It is not the work of life but the worry of life which steals away our strength and finally may prove too much for us. To put it another way, persons seldom work themselves into a nervous breakdown; they worry themselves into it. It is the inner load, not the outer one, which we must learn how to handle.

Unfortunately, many of us try some foolish and futile ways of handling the problem. Some people seem to have the idea that they can "whine it away." But nothing was ever solved or cured by whining and complaining. The result is usually the opposite. Some people imagine they can run away from that inner burden, thinking that a change of location is all they need. They might as well try to get rid of their shadow by a change in scenery. Some people try to make their escape by the tragic way of alcohol or narcotics only to complicate and compound the trouble. Still others keep hoping for some magical medicine or mechanical gadget that will provide the help they need. Whatever relief they find in these directions, however, is usually only temporary.

There must be some way in which men can handle the load of life. There must be a way; or else one of two things is true: Either life itself is a huge cruel joke; or God, the Creator, is a poor architect and engineer.

If man is in a world which can be too much for God, then God failed to calculate correctly the stress and strain which would be placed upon his creatures. For all of his power, he is not much of an engineer; and, from our standpoint, there is not much hope.

I have been caught in several storms while flying and will admit that I am never quite at ease when the plane is being tossed about in the turbulent sky. But the one thought which offers at least some comfort and assurance in the storm is that the engineers who designed the plane and guided its construction knew that such storms would be encountered. They took them into account and built into the plane the strength to withstand the wild winds and turbulence.

Surely God has done the same in his creation. And surely he is as competent as an engineer. The architect of the universe must have known all about the turbulent pressures, the inner burdens, which men might have to bear; he must have planned us equal to the task—provided we would live in a certain way. Nor did he keep the way secret. The trouble is that so many of us do not seek that way or else refuse it.

With the help of three quotations from the New Testament, let us try to define God's way in terms of three principles which will help any one of us to handle the load of our life. They make good sense, good psychology, and good religion.

I

The first principle is *to get rid of some of the load.*

This does not mean that we should try to run out on, or escape from, any responsibility that is rightfully ours to bear. But much of the load that many of us carry is unnecessary; for it is composed of anxious worries and concern over yesterday or tomorrow.

We may need to get rid of some of the past. After all, it is now beyond our power to do anything about yesterday's failures or wrong decisions. We may learn from them, but there is no way to change them. It is foolish, then, to waste the strength we need for today to worry about yesterday. It is better to commit the past to God, trusting in his understanding and his mercy.

Sometimes it is the sense of guilt which bears heavily upon us. We may try to bear it in secret; but, even if we are able to hide it, we cannot hold back the consequences of unforgiven guilt. Some psychiatrists say that back of most mental illness is this burden of guilt. God never intended that we should bear it. We need to get rid of it.

I do not recall where I first read the suggestion that God might be pictured in terms of a divine garbage collector. I remember that, at first, it seemed a sacrilege to think in such terms but, the more I thought about it, the more the picture came to mean. Suppose we tried to keep our garbage in our homes, hiding the scraps and litter away in various parts of the house, day after day, week after week. Think what vermin and disease would poison the entire household, even though the garbage was hidden from the eyes of others. The only answer in a city is for us to arrange for someone to collect it and take it away. The same principle holds in life. If we let the garbage of guilt keep piling up inside of us, trying to hide it away in some dark corner of our consciousness, sooner or later it will work its harm. But God in his forgiveness will take away that garbage and remove this burden of the past which otherwise may break us down.

On the other hand, it may be that we need to get rid of some of the future. If there were some way to measure the total of human energy that is wasted every day in worry about what tomorrow may bring, it would be more than amazing. It would probably be unbelievable. Most of us have our hands full with today's task, and we might be equal to its demands if we did not also try to bear the burden of the future.

In one of his books, Howard Thurmond, a great Negro minister now teaching at Boston University, revealed one secret of how he handled the unusually heavy burdens of his life. It came from a sentence his mother gave him in childhood. Haley's Comet was paying its infrequent visit to the skies above the earth; and, as a little boy, he heard many stories concerning it. Therefore, he begged his mother for permission to stay up late enough to watch the display in the heavens; but she refused and sent him to bed at the regular time. However, during the night, she changed her mind and awakened him, saying, "Come on out in the yard, Howard, and see it."

When he got outside and looked up into the heavens, he saw a frightening, fearful sight. To his childish eyes the stars seemed to be falling. He sought the shelter of his mother's arms and cried, "Mother, what would happen to us if it were to fall and hit us!"

She drew her son close and calmly whispered, "Nothing would happen, Howard. If it were to fall, God would take care of us."

He understood that his mother was not saying that they would be given magical protection. She was saying that no matter what happened, God would take care of them. All through the years of youth and on into adulthood, he remembered those words and often said them over to himself in the face of some fear concerning the future.

It may be that the first step in handling the load of our life involves getting rid of some of it. In this connection we should remember a phrase out of 1 Peter 5:7 which reads, "Cast all your anxieties on him, for he cares about you." Some of the past and some of the future we can commit to the hands of God.

II

The second principle is *to break it up*. The heaviest burden can always be handled if we can break it up into parts.

It is the prerogative of a housewife to decide, every so often, that the furniture must be rearranged and shifted about the room or the house. Most husbands, therefore, know what it is to be greeted, on arriving home, with the announcement that the bookcase must change places with the desk. It involves moving both pieces from one end of the room to the other. Therefore, most of us have learned that it is possible to move a bookcase without permanent back injury if we simply take the books out of it and move them to the new location a few at a time. If we break up the load, we can handle it.

Or suppose we have an appointment with a doctor: we sit in his outer office along with ten other persons. The nurse comes to the door and says, "You may come in now." As we get up, all ten of the others get up and follow us into the doctor's presence. He asks us to be seated and then looking around the circle, he says, "Now tell me, what's your trouble?" We all start talking at once, describing our symptoms. What would happen? Our doctor would soon have to call a doctor for himself. He can give his personal care and attention to each patient one at a time, not all together.

The same thing holds concerning the cares and concerns of life. We can handle almost any burden if we break it up. We can manage a minute. We can handle an hour. We can stand it a day. This is God's plan. We are to live one day at a time. He broke the year to hours and days. The words of George Klingle are often quoted, for they state it clearly:

Should all the weight of life
Be laid across our shoulders, and the future, rife
  With woe and struggle, meet us face to face
    At just one place,
    We could not go;
  Our feet would stop; and so
God lays a little on us every day.

And never, I believe, on all the way
Will burdens bear so deep
Or pathways lie so steep
But we can go, if by God's power,
We only bear the burden by the hour.

III

The third principle is *to share it.*

One of the worst mistakes that we ever make is to let false pride persuade us that there is something courageous or noble in bearing our burdens alone, in hiding them away inside of us. God never intended that we should go it alone: that is why he made us for fellowship and friendship. Everybody needs somebody to talk with, somebody with whom he can share the secret worries and anxious feelings which burden the heart.

We should not go around revealing our heart and talking with just anybody and everybody who will listen. Rather, we should choose some wise and trustworthy friend, a counselor, or our pastor or doctor. We should talk it over with this one and talk it out. There is no principle more essential to handling the load of life than to share it; to keep open the road of communication.

Some idea of the importance of being able to "talk it over" was indicated recently when an authority on family life and marriage said that this breakdown of communication is one of the biggest causes of marriage failure. Husbands and wives simply lose the ability to talk with each other, closing the road of hope.

This ability to "talk it over" is important. A minister went to a home where there had been a suicide. Every member of the family was puzzled; there was seemingly no reason for it. As he sat beside the perplexed and heartbroken wife, she kept saying over and over, "If only he had talked with me about whatever it was, I am sure there would have been some way to handle it, some answer. If only he had talked it over with me." And the tragedy is that she was right. Whatever it was, it probably could have been handled if only he had not tried to bear it alone.

We need to share the inner burden of our life, not only with some trustworthy persons, but also with God. This is one of the great things about praying. "What a privilege to carry everything to him in prayer." I have known persons who tried to withhold from God the truth as if they could hide from him the real trouble in their life.

Prayer is God's great gift to every man. No person needs to go it alone; there is always One with whom we can share it, whatever it is.

I remember a person who was facing a crisis in her life. At first she thought that it was simply more than she could stand. But one morning she said, "I talked it over with God last night, and we can face it!" By "we" she meant God and herself.

In the fourth chapter of Hebrews is the verse we should remember in regard to this principle: "Let us then with confidence draw near to the throne of grace, that we may receive mercy and find grace to help in time of need." (Hebrews 4:16)

We must share it, for God did not intend us to bear it alone.

We can handle the load of life, those inner burdens which bear so heavily upon us, if we will follow the principles revealed in these three verses of Scripture and which we have put into this formula: Let us get rid of some of it. Let us break it up. Let us share it.

Biographical Sketch

Granville T. Walker has served as the pastor of the University Christian Church in Fort Worth, Texas, since 1945. This church is located directly across the street from Texas Christian University, which he attended as an undergraduate and in which he took his seminary training and was later granted the honorary D.D. degree. He took further training at Yale University, receiving the B.D. and Ph.D. degrees from that institution, as well as several honors and awards for scholarship in biblical studies.

Prior to his present position he served as pastor of the St. Charles Avenue Christian Church in New Orleans and, for a time, as chairman of the Department of Undergraduate Religion at T.C.U. He has held many positions of prominence, both denominationally and interdenominationally, including the presidency of the International Convention of Christian Churches.

Dr. Walker has made a lifelong study of the ministry, particularly as it relates to his own communion. He has published one book, *Preaching in the Thought of Alexander Campbell.* He was selected to contribute the chapter on "The Ministry," to a symposium published by the Disciples of Christ, entitled *What We Believe.* In the closing paragraph of this chapter he states his high concept of the ministry:

Some there must be who go into all the world and proclaim the gospel, who are willing to do it as sacrifice of material blessings and for the sake of Him who loved us and gave himself for us. Some there must be who will prepare themselves for the preaching ministry at home, and for whom the ministry will at once be the source of their livelihoods and the object of their deepest dedications. Our conception of the ministry includes the ministry of the laity to be sure, but it must on every count exalt the ministry of those who "live by the gospel," for whom Christian leadership provides their livelihood and being Christian constitutes their lives![1]

Dr. Walker's own ministry is carried on in a university setting. His services each Sunday are filled with students and faculty alike. Of particular interest to this series is the fact

[1]From *What We Believe,* James M. Flanagan, ed. (St. Louis: Bethany Press, 1956), p. 105. Used by permission.

that he is in constant demand as a counselor by students from the campus and people in the community as well. Dr. Elmer Henson, dean of the graduate seminary at Texas Christian University and a member of Dr. Walker's congregation, said of him, "Dr. Walker has a unique ministry to a university community. Whether a student sits in his study for counseling or in the church for worship, he feels that here is a man who understands his problems and speaks to his needs."

This is a sermon which was preached at a time of national crisis, when the newspapers and newscasts filled everyone with tension and uncertainty. So widespread was this feeling throughout the community and the campus that he abandoned the sermon he had prepared and met the occasion with this sermon.

Faith
for a Time of Crisis

BECAUSE OF EVENTS NOW TAKING PLACE over the situation which has developed in Cuba, many people are troubled and justifiably fearful of what may come of it. This situation causes me to change what I had intended to do today on Reformation Sunday, to deal with the question of how Christians may face a time of crisis and alarm when no one knows what a day may bring forth, and when nothing we may do individually except pray can possibly affect the outcome.

For my text I take the words which Jesus uttered to his disciples on the night of the Last Supper, which at all odds was the darkest and most hopeless-appearing moment they ever faced. To use a very descriptive Scottish phrase, "he spoke to their condition" when knowing their feelings of alarm, he said "Let not your heart be troubled: you believe in God, believe also in me."

At that moment the disciples were sorely troubled and filled with dread and apprehension. Jesus had announced that one of them would betray him and that he, himself, would be taken from them and put to death. And the disciples were beginning to realize that the tide of hatred which had been whipped up against Jesus had marooned them in this Upper Room like the rising waters of a flood.

The real peril of their situation had finally dawned upon them. They were alert enough to know that if Jesus were to be crucified as a common criminal, his disciples certainly could not escape. They were fearful then both for him and for themselves. It was in this situation of

113

crisis and alarm that Jesus said to them, "Let not your hearts be troubled; believe in God, believe also in me." (John 14:1)

Surely if Jesus had known a better prescription for their fears than faith in God and in himself he would have offered it. More than that, if he had known of a reasonable way by which, without compromise, the danger could be removed, surely he would have told them of it. Neither was the case. He did not offer them escape but resource; not a way out, but a way through; not some honorable way of retreating from the field of battle, but spiritual armor with which to fight.

Don't let your hearts be troubled, he said. For if you really believe in God, then you do not need to be afraid of those who can "kill the body and after that have no more that they can do." They have no other power over you. They cannot do anything to you or to me which will permanently thwart God's purposes for us. Here, you see, was an answer to their fears which did not try to convince them, falsely, that the worst could not possibly happen—either to himself or to them—but which insisted that if the worst did happen, they had nothing of which to be afraid.

That is a far cry from the false therapies for troubled hearts being "huckstered" to the world today under the guise of good religion. John Macmurray has said that many people in our time "are hag-ridden by fear, 'by the feeling of being alone in a hostile world,' and that a false religion tries to steady them by asserting that what they dread will never really happen—which, says he, is a lie. But a real religion rallies them by convincing them that, if the worst does come, 'there is nothing to be afraid of.' "[2]

Whenever Christianity is represented to you as saying anything else about the fears that haunt us, offering you

[2]*Freedom in the Modern World* (London: Faber & Faber, 1932), pp. 59-60.

escape rather than resource, mark it down that Christ had nothing to do with that.

For Jesus made no false claims about what faith in God and in himself would do. He did not promise that if men really believed in God and were obedient to God's will, the things they feared would be removed or would never happen. He never presented faith as a kind of religious hocus-pocus which can ward off all human hurt, all human tragedy, all human sorrow. On the contrary, he presented faith as the answer with which a believing man can deal with life's most baffling, most heartbreaking and hopeless problems without fear.

Consider the incident recorded in the Gospels when Jesus and his disciples were in a boat on the Sea of Galilee. Jesus, weary from long days and nights of work, was asleep in the boat when a storm arose. His disciples became terribly afraid and awakened him, pleading that he do something about it. And stilling the storm—both the storm within their hearts and the storm without—he said to them, "Why are you afraid, O men of little faith?" Their faith, as Jesus saw it, was not intended to keep the storm from hitting, nor would it have kept them from getting hurt if it did. Their faith was not to keep them from being hurt but from being afraid. "After all," he says in effect, "our lives are in the hands of God. We are not alone. God is with us." With that confidence, what one is delivered from is not the storm, but fear of the storm.

What I am saying now ought to be of considerable importance to most of us in this house this morning. Often when facing with someone a real and distressing problem, the quite heart-rending statement is heard, "Why has God allowed this to happen to us? We have prayed. We have believed in his goodness. We have tried to be good ourselves. But surely something we have done has been wrong!"

The illness of a loved one, or some tragic accident, is looked upon as a fearsome punishment for something one has done, he knows not what. It would not have happened (so he for the moment argues) if he had had faith enough, or if he had done something he had left undone, or not done something which he did. Thus, added to the awful thing, is a still worse thing—a terrible sense of unforgiven guilt. Belief in God, far from alleviating the anxiety, has deepened it.

If calling upon your faith in God in the moment of crisis makes matters worse instead of better, then you would do well to take another look at the God you worship. What kind of God would God be if he would strike a child down with polio in order to punish a father or a mother? Could you possibly trust a God like that? Of course you could not trust a God like that.

You cannot trust a God who is not trustworthy. No one could trust a God who, because someone had failed to do any particular thing, would punish another person in order to take vengeance on the guilty party. What manner of beastly God would do this? No, my friend, when your faith in God makes matters worse instead of better, there is something wrong with the God you worship.

Jesus believed that God is a god in whom you can trust. When he said to his disciples, "You believe in God" he meant, knowing what you know to be true about God, then trust him to see matters through to the end—beyond the horizon which is the limit of your sight.

That may be why Jesus having said, "Let not your hearts be troubled; believe in God," added the phrase, "believe also in me." What could he possibly have meant by that, except that as we look upon Jesus Christ and believe in him, we then are enabled to believe in his God, faith in whom delivers us from our fears.

Here is the secret of faith which is the victory that overcomes the world, namely, that because the God we worship is like Christ, we can without fear, whatever happens, trust him with ourselves and our loved ones in both life and death.

Leslie Weatherhead in his little book, *Prescription for Anxiety,* has a chapter with the intriguing title, "The Truth About God Lessens Anxiety." That title is worth pondering—the *truth* about God lessens anxiety. Not some childish picture about God which you never outgrew— a composite picture "made out of stern parents, angry school teachers, or fierce denunciatory preachers with an added element of a great big policeman, Gestapo official, or angry potentate,"[3] not the picture of God with the record of your life and conduct in one hand and a club raised to strike you at the first opportunity in the other. Do you think that trust in such a God would lessen your fears? Far from it, it would make matters worse instead of better.

No, it is the truth about God—as revealed in Christ— which delivers us when by faith we appropriate that truth into our lives. What kind of God do we Christians really worship? In John's Gospel, in the same chapter from which our text is taken, Jesus says, "He who has seen me has seen the Father." Which is to say that the God we trust who delivers us, not from danger, but from the fear of danger, not from death, but from the fear of death, is like Christ. This is the noblest thing we can say of God, the thing that emancipates us from our fears, cutting us loose from the bondage of our anxieties, namely, that we cannot ascribe to our God any behavior which we would not be willing to ascribe to Christ. Believe in God; believe also in me.

Further, the truth about God which lessens our fears when we trust him is that God loves us all unconditionally. It is this which Jesus reveals most fully about God—

---

[3] Leslie D. Weatherhead, *Prescription for Anxiety* (Nashville: Abingdon Press), p. 45.

that his love for us is not conditioned upon our moral perfection, though he himself wants us to be perfect, even as the father is perfect. Even so the love of the father continues to follow the prodigal all the way to the far country, even to the degradation of the pig pen, and it is the father's love which finally wins him back. Here is the truth about God which people find it hardest, apparently, to accept; namely that God's love for all of us or any of us does not in any given moment rest back upon our attainment of some moral standard. The glorious truth is that God loves us whatever we do. Under no condition do we ever deserve God's love, but it is always there whether we be clean or dirty, kind or brutal, good or bad.

Jesus insisted on this time and again: The Father, he declared, "makes his sun rise on the evil and on the good, and sends rain on the just and on the unjust." "Love your enemies," says Jesus, "and pray for those who persecute you, so that you may be sons of your Father who is in heaven." And Paul caught the great import of that same unconditional and impartial love of God when he said, "God shows his love for us in that while we were yet sinners Christ died for us!" I have not said this to encourage anyone in his evil. Far from it! I assume I am talking to people, who more than anything else, want to follow Christ and be like Christ.

In any case, this kind of love will make us good instead of evil if we respond to it. But I have said it to say this: This is the kind of God whom we can trust in a time of crisis, in a time of trouble, in a time of danger, in a time of alarm, or even as was the case of the disciples, when death threatens to invade the circle of our loves. If his willingness to deliver us from our fears depended upon any moral attainment we could claim, we would never, any of us, be delivered and we know it. It depends only on our readiness to turn to him in faith.

Turning to God for help in a moment of need, and getting it has been a turning point in many a life. Harry Emerson Fosdick in his autobiography recounts the great crisis of a nervous breakdown which came to him in his early seminary days. The whole experience, horrid as it was, he says was one of the most important factors in his preparation for the ministry. For the first time in his life and at his wit's end, he faced a situation which was too much for him to handle. Listen to his own description:

I went down into the depths where self-confidence becomes ludicrous. There the technique I had habitually relied upon— marshaling my wit and my volition and going strenuously after what I wanted—petered completely out. The harder I struggled, the worse I was. It was what I did the struggling with that was sick. I, who had thought myself strong, found myself beaten, unable to cope not only with outward circumstances but even with myself. In that experience I learned some things about religion that theological seminaries do not teach. I learned to pray, not because I had adequately argued out prayer's rationality, but because I desperately needed help from a Power greater than my own. I learned that God, much more than a theological proposition, is an immediately available Resource; that just as around our bodies is a physical universe from which we draw all our physical energy, so around our spirits is a spiritual Presence in living communion with whom we can find sustaining strength.[4]

That, I take it, is one of the most important lessons great religion has to teach—a lesson caught up in Jesus' simple admonition: "Let not your hearts be troubled; believe in God, believe also in me."

---

[4]Fosdick, *The Living of These Days*, p. 75.

PART II

Bring Good Tidings

Sermons preached by specialists in pastoral care

> The Spirit of the Lord GOD is upon me,
>   because the LORD has anointed me
> to bring good tidings to the afflicted;
>   he has sent me to bind up the brokenhearted,
> to proclaim liberty to the captives,
>   and the opening of the prison to those who
>   are bound;
> to proclaim the year of the LORD's favor,
>   and the day of vengeance of our God;
>   to comfort all who mourn;
> to grant to those who mourn in Zion—
>   to give them a garland instead of ashes,
> the oil of gladness instead of mourning,
>   the mantle of praise instead of a faint
>   spirit. . . .

—Isaiah 61:1-3

> " '. . . as you did it to one of the least of
>   these my brethren, you did it to me.' "

—Matthew 25:40

When Jesus spoke in the synagogue in Nazareth, he selected this passage from Isaiah to read as a description of his ministry and his mission. This could be selected as a passage to guide the aims of the pastoral care movement, "to bring good tidings to the afflicted," "to bind up the brokenhearted," "proclaim liberty to the captives," "to give them a garland instead of ashes." The sermons in this section were all prepared by men who have specialized in the field of pastoral care. Some are professors, some are chaplains of institutions, some have made special studies in certain areas such as older persons or the home. These men are also preachers. Most of them served as pastors before becoming professors or chaplains. They all continue to preach, in local churches, in chapel services, on special occasions, and, in the case of the chaplains, regularly before a congregation of people with special needs. They all have a unique background which enables them to relate the insights found in pastoral care to the task of preaching.

Biographical Sketch

WAYNE OATES

Wayne Oates is the Professor of Psychology of Religion at Southern Baptist Seminary, Louisville, Kentucky, and serves frequently as visiting professor of pastoral counseling at Union Theological Seminary in New York.

He began his study of human relations when he was a page in the United States Senate. He graduated from Wake Forest College where he later returned to teach philosophy and psychology. He received his Theological training at Duke Divinity School and Southern Baptist Seminary where he received his Th.D. degree.

Dr. Oates has held pastorates in North Carolina and Kentucky and served as chaplain of the Kentucky State Hospital. He has been one of the most productive writers in the field. Many of his books, such as *The Christian Pastor, Religious Factors in Mental Illness, The Bible in Pastoral Care, Anxiety in Christian Experience, Christ and Selfhood,* and *Protestant Pastoral Counseling,* are considered required reading in most seminaries.

He is in almost constant demand for lectures before ministers' institutes and seminaries throughout the country. He speaks and writes from a rich background of wide experience and continued study. In all his work he combines the practical applications of the experienced pastor with the theological content and orientation of the scholar.

In the midst of all this activity of teacher, scholar, author, lecturer, counselor, he has continued to be a most effective preacher. In a recent volume of sermons *The Revelation of God in Human Suffering,* from which we have quoted elsewhere in this book, he said of his own preaching, "I speak as a preacher who is committed, as much as in me lies, to proclaim 'the whole counsel of God.'" Speaking of the relationship of preaching and pastoral work, he said,

Counseling, psychology, and psychology of religion as implemented by a Christian pastor are inseparable from the work he does as a preacher. . . . A very real difference between these two ministries of the pastor exists alongside equally important similarities. When the preacher preaches, he appeals to the common and more universal

123

elements in the human situation, whereas the pastoral counselor is committed to discovering the unique individuality of one person at a time and what the universals mean to him.[1]

Here, in this sermon, is an example of how he speaks to one of the "universals" of our day combining both psychological and sociological data with a thorough knowledge of Scripture. He describes its background in these words:

> This sermon was preached in two particular places —New York and Washington. The reason I chose this sermon for these two places was the terrible sense of unrootedness which I find in both places. They have many people who have lived there for years who still think of some place else as their home. In Washington, this is symbolized by the necessity of every Washingtonian to vote by absentee ballot in an election. This uprootedness leads to a "detached" way of life that avoids covenant-making that will lead to durable relationships.
>
> Furthermore, the nerve of the missionary outreach of the church is based in the mind and intention of God to transcend the "local deities" of contemporary cultural religions. This challenges idolatry directly. The "detached motif is approached indirectly and winsomely because such behavior is rooted in painful experiences of persons with family, neighbor, and home community. Many of them are like Thomas Wolfe—they "can't go home again." Therefore, they must be dealt with tenderly, compassionately, and indirectly. But the deification of "things back home" is a steadfast and conscious refusal to grow. This must be confronted head on. Both these things I deal with in these moods.
>
> It seems to me that the mobility of people today is a factor much deplored but little understood and appreciated from the pulpit of today. The conscious

---

[1]From *The Revelation of God in Human Suffering* by Wayne Oates. © 1959, W. L. Jenkins. The Westminster Press.

effort to appreciate is a part of vital preaching and a necessary precondition to being heard on more sensitive issues. One of the objectives of this sermon, therefore, is to project oneself into the harassed conditions of the urban dweller today, to feel as he feels, and to communicate hope and light for his way.

The Need for Roots

THE JEWS HAD BEEN TAKEN AS CAPTIVES OF WAR. They were carried into Babylon, torn from the roots of their existence in their native land. The ground of their identity had been torn from beneath them. Now they were in strange territory. One of their poets wrote:

By the waters of Babylon, there we sat down and wept
    when we remembered Zion.
On the willows there
        we hung up our lyres.
For there our captors
        required of us songs,
    and our tormentors, mirth, saying;
        "Sing us one of the songs of Zion!"

How shall we sing the LORD's song
    in a foreign land?

—Psalm 137:1-4

In these last words: "How shall we sing the LORD's song in a foreign land?" the Hebrew poet stated the dilemma of all religious people of all times who have been uprooted from their native soil. To what extent did their religion depend upon the soil in which it was rooted. What happens to a person's religious faith when he is no longer in his native country?

This is an imperative dilemma for you and me, for our families, and for our churches today. One out of four families will change its address this coming year, and change its address from one state of the union to another or to a foreign country. The exceptional mobility of life today, also, is not merely geographical. Persons who live in the same city all their lives will tend to change their social group. They move up or down the social ladder in such a way that the religious group of their youth will not be the spiritual community of their adulthood. A process of uprooting, transplanting, and all these hazards that go with it takes place. By social change, they will often be uprooted through education and occupation from the religion of their parents. They are faced with social uprooting in the same way that others are confronted with geographical uprooting. In many instances, both kinds of both social and geographical moving take place in the lives of the same persons.

Uprooting and transplanting is a part of life. It must be faced. Abraham went out by faith from Ur of the Chaldees. The very nature of marriage itself causes man and woman, if they live according to God's purpose in creation, to leave father and mother and cleave to one another. As they grow older and their own children mature, they in turn have their nest torn up by the education, vocation, and marriage of their children. Furthermore, the stern injunction of the Lord Jesus Christ is that the easy securities of houses, lands, husbands, wives, children, mothers, and fathers are to be left for the greater security of rootage in the kingdom of God. Then and only then does life come into true fruitage.

In the face of the dilemmas of uprooting, people are called upon to "sing the song of their God" in strange lands. The dangers and possibilities of this uprooting in the spiritual life were the burden of concern of the poet who wrote the first Psalm. Briggs rightly translates Psalm 1:6 "He is like a tree that is *transplanted* by streams of water, that yields its fruit in its season, and its leaf does not wither. In all that he does he prospers." Yet before the psalmist comes to this mood of affirmation, he recognizes that not all men are so. Some remain unrooted. They wither, dry, remain fruitless, and are like the chaff that the wind blows away.

The fact remains that much of our religion depends upon having an environment conducive to its growth and nurture. The burden of our text is: "Does our faith in God depend *entirely* upon that conducive evironment of our hometown?" "Are the sons of Zion applicable *only* in the friendly territory of Zion itself?" Can we stand the shock of uprooting? The validity of our faith is tested in this shock. Plato tells the story of the Shepherd of Gyges, a young shepherd who found a ring which would make him invisible to his neighbors. This gave him the right to do as he pleased without being observed or detected. Prior to his having received this ring, he was a righteous, godly, and virtuous man. After he was freed of the scrutinizing eyes and detecting influence of his neighbors, he became an unscrupulous, ungodly, and rapacious man. This is what Albert Camus described as "achieving more than the vulgar ambitious man and rising to that supreme summit where virtue is its own reward." The reward for such virtue is the adulation of one's associates. We are told that religion at its best is what a man does in his solitude, how he handles his aloneness before God. Herein is a major test of his faith. When one is uprooted from his provincial surroundings, no longer has to report in to mother and father, husband and/or wife, neighbor and friend, he confronts himself afresh as he really is. The conventional, routine, and habitual sources of his faith are torn away. He becomes what he really is, not what he seems to be or would like to appear to be. Otherwise courteous, unselfish, and gentle people often become rude, grasping, and harsh people when the secondary gains of approval of a known fellowship of their own personal Zion is no longer about to reward them for goodness.

On the other hand, uprooting may simply overtake some, not with actual wrongdoing, but with homesickness, bereavement, and self-pity. Uprooting is particularly hard on little children and young people who are developing their sense of identity in relation to their chums and fellow schoolmates. One friend of mine in Washington—which is a city of displaced persons—moved from one side of the city to the other. It disrupted his seven-year-old son's play and school groups. He was very sad. He asked his father if they might not have a prayer room in their new home, because, he said: "We need a prayer room for times like these."

Many of us, though, as adults, do not work through our grief in fear and trembling and prayer. We simply deify the religion of our home province. We assume that there are no other places like the old places, no ways to worship others than the way they worship "back home," no songs but the songs of Zion with which to sing glad praise to God. We react as Naaman did when the prophet Elisha healed him. He thought that *only* the two mules' burdens of earth upon which he had originally encountered God, his first healing experience of grace, could provide adequate nourishment for his spiritual life. He asked to take this dirt back to Syria with him. Like him, we would haul our geography around with us in our minds' eyes and never test the new soil upon which we are standing, never assess the streams of water around us for their sustaining powers for spiritual growth. We may be so impressed with the Mississippi River, the Wabash River, the Sewanee River, the Missouri River, or the Jordan River, that the Hudson River and the East River and the Harlem River or the Ohio River only cause us to weep for home.

Gross rebellion and idolatrous grief, then, are two of the negative possibilities of uprooting. But the psalmist speaks of rerooting, *transplanting* as the better way. The psalmist meditated upon the law of the Lord both day and night. He discovered in the new land of Babylon streams of living water. He rerooted himself in the spiritual subsoil of his new environment. When we follow his example, we can stand the shock of transplantation. We can make a living contribution to the community of which we are newly become a part. At the same time, we begin to discover new things about ourselves and about the nature of God himself.

The most important thing I suppose we learn about ourselves is that we are more akin to all mankind than we are estranged from and different from all mankind. As Harry Stack Sullivan says, we are more distinctly human than otherwise. The West Coast person who grew up in a community where Orientals were a threat discovers, for example, a kinship with them in New York that he did not know before. As one little Japanese boy playing with a child from a white family said: "I can't play war with my friend. He and I know each other too well. We have to go out and find some people we don't know so well to play war with and to play like we are shooting them." A Southerner from Alabama who has accustomed herself to thinking of Negroes as uneducated and uncommunicative is jarred in her presuppositions about the Negro race as a whole based upon her limited experience. Or a New Yorker visiting in Mississippi will discover that not all Mississippians are members of a hate-venting mob. The Britisher who comes to America thinking of all Americans as affluent worshipers of the almighty dollar is shaken to discover an American social worker who eats a slim helping at the local Chock-Full-o'-Nuts and shares her funds liberally in order that her young charges might have the privilege of a religious ministry they otherwise would not get. Even in hurdy-gurdy, glittering New York, impersonal as the subway population would maskedly have you believe it is, there quietly emerges a kinship system, a fellowship that is unorganized but effective, quiet but deeply penetrating. It nourishes the roots of the life of the person who will let his roots stay in one place long enough to be fed aright.

If we learn this about ourselves, then, during times of uprooting, the most important thing we learn about God is that God is not restricted to our home place. He is not too high and lifted up to become a Nazarene, but at the same time, he is Spirit. Those who worship him must worship him, not on one mountain or another mountain, neither on Gerizim nor in Jerusalem, but in Spirit and in truth. He is the God

> who stretches out the heavens like a curtain,
>   and spreads them like a tent to dwell in.

He cannot be contained in any load of earth that two mules can pull. God is not another Britisher, nine feet tall. God is not a Southern plantation owner. God is in New York, but New Jersey is not west nor Boston east to him. This is the great discovery the Jews made in the Exile: that God was not just in Zion, that one did not have to be in Zion to sing songs of praise and worship to him. This was the discovery about God they brought back from the Exile!

These are the two things I hope we will discover as we worship quietly in our places. Right around us here in this city, in this church, we can find both soil and springs of spiritual reality whereby we may take root and grow in this community of faith. We may be alone and isolated, separated from our enduring community of faith, but here on the very ground upon which we stand God is ready and willing to reveal to us people of good will, of lasting devotion, and spiritual integrity to whom we can be related. We need not forever be spiritual tumbleweeds, cast about by every wind that blows. We need not be spiritually unproductive though we are here for only a little while. The simple fact remains that none of us has a lasting dwelling place in time. The very nature of life itself is to uproot and transplant itself in order to be productive and reproductive. This is the missionary impulse and nerve of the life of the Christian community. We need not always be a guest in this church. This can be a place where we can sing a new song to the Lord. We can find sustenance, renewal, and spiritual rootage in faith here in worship.

We are a flying people who take the wings of the morning and literally fly to the uttermost parts of the sea. Yet we cannot fly away from God ever. We always fly to God. Even in our most extended journey, God is our dwelling place from everlasting to everlasting. If we make our bed in hell, he is there. Both darkness and light are alike to him. He is the ground of our being and the source of our kinship systems. We need not be lost sheep of the house of Israel because we are uprooted. We need not wither and become chaff for the wind to blow away in our self-pity, nostalgia, and separation from the accustomed environment of our home province. We need not be orphans, for God, upon the request of Jesus Christ, wills to give us the Holy Spirit. Thus we can be uprooted and transplanted. We can bring forth fruit in due season without a leaf withering.

We thank thee for the godly fellowship of the Christian faith upon which the sun never sets nor fails to rise each morning. We thank thee for thy eternal presence, that thou art always nigh. Root us and ground us in love that we may bring forth fruit in thy name.

Amen.

Biographical Sketch

THOMAS W. KLINK

Thomas W. Klink is a Methodist minister, currently chaplain and coordinator of graduate studies in religion and psychiatry at The Menninger Foundation, Topeka, Kansas. Born in New York state, educated in Oregon and at the University of Chicago, his ministry has centered in a variety of correctional, medical, and psychiatric institutions. He is an accredited supervisor and has been president of the Council for Clinical Training.

He is highly qualified to speak on the problem of preaching in a mental hospital setting. He gives a background for his sermon in the following paragraphs.

In 1960 more than a half-million people were in public psychiatric hospitals. These facilities counted 192,000 admissions during the year; 143,000 persons were discharged; 46,000 died in hospitals. In nearly every institution some form of religious ministry is carried on, most universally public worship and preaching. The potential "congregation" for preaching in psychiatric hospitals is approximately the same number as the total population of Seattle, Indianapolis, Minneapolis, or Atlanta.

What are the life situations to which preaching must address itself in these congregations? What influences shape religious needs of psychiatric patients in addition to general needs that may be deduced from the broad fact of psychiatric illness? How may preaching be conceived so as to contribute to the resources which psychiatric patients can mobilize to cope with their life situations? The sermon below is chosen to illustrate a few of the answers to these questions.

Kiekegaard (in *Discourses on Emergent Occasions*) and Martin Buber have demonstrated a mode of communication marked by *direct address in identity*. This style of speaking is peculiarly relevant to the life situation of the psychiatric patient.

Mental illness may be marked by gross confusion of identity. The experience of hospitalization invariably separates patients from the supporting web of relations in which the sense of identity is normally maintained—home, job, friends, church. Persons whose life stresses have forced the use of psychiatric symptoms are, most often, individuals least strongly embedded in a stable sense of the self—identity. Rennie and his associates, in the cross-section study of an urban population, report on the massive contemporary assaults on this sense of identity. They call it a pressure towards "anomie." Thus, a sermon in our times—and especially in the psychiatric hospital—must deal with persons stressed in their identity. One way of speaking to this need is to adopt the mode of direct address, speaking to the congregation in the immediately present circumstances of hospitalization. My point may be made in the profane (but here expurgated) words of a prisoner following the preaching of a visiting parson, "Either he was shy, stupid, or scared. I don't want to go to chapel and have my nose rubbed into it, but I do want to hear somebody preach who shows that he is aware that I'm in jail."

Like nearly everybody I have a watch that occasionally needs cleaning or repair. When that happens, I wear out my bare wrist, aware only because of its absence, how many times a day I check the time. The psychiatric patient may be severely disoriented in time, not knowing day, month, or year. Some observers have noted that acutely disturbed patients are victims of a disturbed sense of time—for example, they recall a painful past event and the anxiety overwhelms them as powerfully as though the event were still occurring. They are unprotected in the present from the past by a stable internalized chronology. Further, some persons—and many of these become psychiatric patients—are subject to significant memory disturbances. This problem is especially troublesome for persons suffering the effects of aging. In any case, admission to a "total institution," like a psychiatric hospital or prison, means entering a different "time zone." The routines of the day and the week are different from those "outside." There are many individual crises but the periodization of time—by Sundays, holidays, special events, unique meals, etc. —is almost inevitably washed out by institutional routine. If the experience with the absent wrist watch is indicative, the loss or flattening out of time is a critical matter. To this need regular worship and preaching can speak, enhancing the effect of the progression of the weeks and the year, binding feelings to a distinctive time other than allowing them to "free float."

Specifically related to the need for time aids are the needs related to great holidays. "Old-timers' wisdom" must always be taken with a grain of salt. Yet, almost invariably, hospital-wise employees recall that "We get our worst patients at Christmas" or "Holy Week seems to upset the patients," etc. These central religious holy days are usually thought of as times of joyous festivity or solemn celebration. More than at any other time we are tempted—observing filled pews from the pulpit—to assume that such days are universally joyful. Even in the hospital there are special efforts by staff, and volunteers for those remaining in hospital. An increasingly large number do go home. Despite these facts the old-timers' phrases have a ring of verisimilitude—that might reach beyond the hospital gate. The ring of credibility is derived from a universal psychological condition—ambivalence, or mixed and contrary feelings about important objects or beloved ones. If preaching is to speak to life situations, it must voice such mixed feelings—love dominant but intertwined with hate; anticipation alloyed with anxiety, achievement tempered by the sense of things undone. Grandiloquent homiletic oratory, extolling in glowing terms the familiarly loved objects, may be justified at times. It may be dismissed, at least, as doing no harm. In the psychiatric hospital, however, where repression of negative feelings is an endemic disease and where ambivalences tend to be more delicately poised, such "positive preaching" can be positively destructive. The sermon that follows was chosen to illustrate the need to preach, with the Apostle Paul, to human experience of "good that would" and "evil that would not."

Finally, it should be noted that the psychiatric patient distrusts his experiences. The stress of irruptive, long-repressed feelings has made him unsure of his experience as a guide to living. His recourse to symptoms may be understood as reflecting his attempt to renounce experience as meaningful. In his flight from the relevance of experience, the psychiatric patient throws into sharper relief the more universal human condition. Thus, the sermon is an occasion for the preacher to use the authority of the gospel to reinforce the meaningfulness of human experience as confirmed by the genotypical accounts of the scriptures. The holiday seasons—occasions hollowed out of the tradition as especially universal—provide the opportunity for the preacher to reinforce the universal in his congregation's experiences; separating such from the idiosyncratic individual.

Out
of the Ordinary

TODAY IS THE SUNDAY NEAREST CHRISTMAS. We do not know for sure when Christ was born. We celebrate his birthday on December 25 but there is no clear statement of the date or time of year on which Joseph and Mary made the weary trek from Nazareth to Bethlehem. Despite this absence of clear guidance, the Christian folk have celebrated this blessed event on or very near to December 25 since the third century. Thereby hangs a story.

We will celebrate the birth of Christ next Sunday because of the ancient peoples' understanding of the calendar. They, like us, noted the fact of the winter solstice in these short days. They may not have understood that they observed the result of the earth's increased distance from the sun. They did not fail to note what has intruded into our experience these last few days—the dark in the room when the ward awakens in the morning, the early descending dusk at suppertime.

If we had never noticed the facts before, we might be alarmed but we have been through this many years before. We know from our experience that out of the increasing darkness there will come a turning, a lengthening of the day and a growth in the light. It was this very experience that contributed to the early Christian's practice of celebrating the birth of Christ in this season: Out of the darkness of a rude place, a stable, there came an infant cry and, in that moment, light began to dawn in swelling proportions again.

137

It is not strange that the two great Christian festivals should be determined not alone by history but by the seasons—Christmas at the winter solstice and Easter in the spring. The fact tells us what we can, in small measure, know in our experience, that out of ordinary events of our lives, trusted to be worthy of notice, there can be seen a promise of the turning which is hope. Let us say this again, in a different way.

There was darkness in the December night of the year 1492. Three tiny ships had pushed out into the darkness of an unknown sea bound for they knew not where. Some saw their voyage as a search for ancient lands of rich treasure. Through the months and the days of the fall the *Santa Maria*, the *Nina*, and the *Pinta* westered. They sailed uncharted seas. We have known what such explorations cost in feelings. Finally, ahead of them was land! Eagerness, competition, skills grown rusty in the long months of running before the wind, sheer misfortune—whatever the cause the anxious mariners sailed the awkward *Nina* straight into shallow surf water and, before they were all ashore, the vessel was broken up in the sea. Thus it was that the first Christmas in America was spent with despair tempering joy. They were in a strange place. One of three fragile ties to home had been lost. The land was interesting but as yet unexplored. It was in this mood that the first Christmas in the New World was spent. The diary of the priestly companion of the voyage, *las Casas*, tells what happened. There on the shore, around the campfires, they ate and, as the vesper benedictions died, they turned to one of the familiar miracle plays of the Spanish countryside. In despair they re-enacted the scene of the Bethlehem stable, playing the parts of the mother and father, shepherds, wise men. The diary tells the result in words that can echo our feelings: "We felt strangely transported out of our troubles into hope." Out of the ordinary stuff of a seashore, firelight, food, and companionship in difficulties the familiar miracle was evoked. The darkness of despair did not lift into full brightness any more than the Christ was born full-grown. Instead it was like the experience of this season. Hope came out of a sense of a turning in the balance of light and dark with the tide changing the smallest, most tentative bit toward a flood of new life.

Today is the Sunday before Christmas. Again, in the different setting of the hospital we experience the deepest of the year's darkness. But in this very season we can also experience the first shadings and lengthenings of the light in the midst of darkness. Think with me about some of the meanings of this for us here in this place, today: how holiness may be found in the midst of the ordinary.

Each of us who come to this place on this Sunday morning comes from the individual ways of our separate lives. But the gospel of hope in Jesus Christ is a universal one. It speaks to all men and women in all conditions of life. Yet it speaks most clearly when it addresses us in our particular individual circumstances. It addresses each of us in the fullness of our personal lives. Remember Zacchaeus. He was up a tree. He was on the outside of the crowd around Jesus. He was a face in a small sea of faces. Jesus' words were not to the crowd in their generality; they were to Zacchaeus, "Zacchaeus, make haste and come down; for I must stay at your house today." Isaiah, on walls of Jerusalem with King Ahaz spoke in this same vein in the prophecy that we read this morning, "Take heed . . ." and went on to note the most ordinary thing of the experience of men, "a young woman shall conceive and bear a son . . . before the child knows how to refuse the evil and choose the good," the threat of the day will have passed. The gospel speaks to each of us in our joys and despairs, our achievements and our problems.

For some of you this has been a season of more than darkness in the sky. Some of you worship with us here for the first time. You are filled with the busyness of the events that, willingly or under duress, brought you to this place. You have been forced by others or by an awareness of need to separate from familiar circumstances. Perhaps only now in this moment is there opportunity to pause and reflect, separating the days, one from another, assorting to each their events, their different feelings, the changes of inner experience bound to the chain of time. Familiar acquaintances have been left behind and new companions intrude into the most personal aspects of living. For some of you this has been a time in which the events have left you very much alone. Yet, reach out of the lonely darkness for a moment and recall the ordinary events whose Fruit we celebrate. They were lifted up from home, too. It was not convenient to follow the Caesar's decree and travel, certainly not with Mary already far advanced in her pregnancy, Joseph already distraught with the anxieties of all fathers of first-born children. And then in the inn or, rather, the stable cave was little privacy, little protection from the intrusion of interested but alien visitors—shepherds, wise men, other travelers. Yet out of this ordinary experience there came holiness.

For some of you these weeks have been times of venturing. You have laid hold in thought of your life, its limitations and its patterns. You have seen how that which you seek lies close at hand. For some of you these days have been times of narrowing in, like a mother approaching the time of delivery. You have found familiar interests insignificant. You have found the focus of life narrowed down to within yourself. But now is the time of birth—and the season becomes symbolic of what is individually true without regard to the calendar; that which has occupied your energy is no longer a creature within. It is a life set free into independent existence and we shudder to recapture the sense of autonomous integrity.

Some of the rest of us have experienced these days as new units in the inexorable course of events activated by our personal history. Like the spinning of a top we have reconfirmed our feeling that there is nothing left in our hands except the endurance of watching the spinning motion run down. We are old and, in our way, cynical hands. We have seen "them" come and go—and the "them" means new staff, new patients, new programs. We are not moved. We have a room in the inn and no claims from the stable will move us. It is not much of an inn but we were checked in first. And yet, even to us this gospel, and this season's experiences which are its form, speak. For new life has come into our midst and we must respond. This Christ, confirmed in the promise of the lengthened day, cannot be casually dismissed. He demands notice—not overwhelmingly like those from whom we have so long fled—but compellingly, drawing out of our own selves the assent.

Anxiety, yes. The Christ whose coming we celebrate calls us to take up a larger share. Loneliness, no. The circumstances of his coming remind us that the way we travel is not untrodden, for this was his name, Immanuel, God-is-with-us.

In the days that come, we will go apart. Some of us will stay here. Some of us will be propelled by the urgency of the season and our own tentative readiness into travel. We will go home.

It is not easy to go home when one has fled or been taken from there in fear. Yet we will go, in anxiety and trembling. We will meet familiar faces who will reflect lack of understanding. We may meet a sensitive one or two who, not comfortable with their sensitivity, will understand. But recall, in hospital or afar, that it is not their understanding that confirms to God our experience. It is Christ whose coming confirms us, as it did those long ago in their capacity to seize control of history and remake it, by grace, in the measure of his image which he shall grant to us. Let us pray.

Almighty God, this is not an easy time for us. We cherish fond memories. We are racked by known and unknown terrors. The darkness settles, or has settled, or is close. O God, the Light, grant us the sure knowledge that the Light is not of our kindling, but of thine; that it will endure until our readiness. Forgive us our reluctance to turn to it. In Christ's name, Amen.

Biographical Sketch

GRANGER WESTBERG

Granger Westberg has the unique distinction of serving on the faculty of a medical school and a theological school at the same time. He was ordained into the Lutheran ministry in 1939. He served for five years as the pastor of St. John's Parish in Bloomington, Illinois. Then he served for eight years as the chaplain of Augustana Hospital in Chicago. In 1952 he accepted a call to become chaplain of the University of Chicago and to teach in the theological school. At the present time he is Associate Professor of Religion and Health at the University of Chicago, with responsibility for the training of both doctors and pastors.

Throughout his career he has been a real pioneer in the interrelationship of religion and medicine. He has worked to improve chaplaincy services in hospitals and was one of the organizers of the American Association of Protestant Hospital Chaplains. He speaks frequently before both medical societies and ministerial associations on the necessity of a team-approach.

He has published two books which deal specifically with this subject. *Nurse, Pastor and Patient* was written to help the nurse understand the spiritual implications of her task and to work more cooperatively with the pastor. As the title implies, *Minister and Doctor Meet*, a Pastoral Psychology Book Club Selection, was written to help the doctor and the minister understand each other and to indicate how they can work together for the good of the patient, both in body and in spirit.

Here he presents a meditation prepared for a service in a hospital and also a statement of principles to guide those who are called upon to do this type of preaching.

Conducting a Sunday morning service in a typical general hospital chapel offers the preacher an opportunity to speak to an unusually ecumenical congregation. Even a group of only thirty to fifty patients

143

usually represents a cross section of the community. This means that these people hold a variety of attitudes toward the church and some belong to no church and are not contemplating joining one. They have come to the hospital chapel because a nurse or a friend has encouraged them to do so. They are going through a difficult period in their own life and are wondering if perhaps this experience might prove helpful. This chapel service has been represented to them as a part of the hospital's therapeutic service and so they go with a fairly open mind about it.

It is impossible to reach, in any deep sense, all of the types of people who attend such a service. However, our experience has been that the people who attend are in a receptive frame of mind—more so than a typical congregation in the same community. Even though the hospital patient may be quite critical of the church when he is outside and well, he responds with unexpected enthusiasm to any evidence of warmth and concern on the part of the pastor or chaplain in charge of the service. People who find themselves hospital patients often listen to the sermon with a new eagerness, hoping that it will somehow speak to their particular needs. The preacher should not attempt anything too long or complicated but rather seek to be somewhat conversational yet presenting a realistic interpretation of the kinds of life problems which these patients are most likely to be facing and to which the Christian faith can speak. The whole service should be set in the context of hope and everything should point to the assurance that God is a very present help in time of trouble.

My feeling has always been that 30 minutes is about all that hospital patients can be expected to be able to sit still. This means that the sermon would be beween 8 and 12 minutes in length. We have found that when patients are told in advance the length of the service they feel more relaxed about going.

> *"And he made from one every nation of men to live on all the face of the earth, . . . that they should seek God. . . . Yet he is not far from each one of us, for*
> *'In him we live and move and have our being.'"*
> —Acts 17:26-28

A Hospital Meditation

We welcome you to this service this morning and know that for many of you this is a different kind of worship experience, for it is probably the first time you have ever attended a worship service in your pajamas. Undoubtedly because of this you had some hesitation about coming here when you were invited by one of the nurses or a volunteer. Somehow we are all in the habit of thinking that the only way we can worship God is to attend our church in our "Sunday-go-to-meeting" clothes and when it is proposed that we attend a service without being all dressed up, we feel a little guilty to appear before God in something less than our best attire. There is much good to be said for being "dressed in our best" and "at our best" in the presence of God. But there is also much to be said for being able to worship God even when we are at our worst or dressed in anything but our Sunday best. God has said, "Lo, I am with you always," which means wherever you are, however you are dressed, and in whatever situation you find yourself. God wants you to feel at ease in his presence.

A second difference about this hospital chapel service is that we seldom have the opportunity to worship with a group of people who represent so many different denominations, both Catholic and Protestant. There is some unusual drawing power which has brought us together into this room today. We are a group of people who come from a variety of backgrounds yet we all have one thing in common—God is our Father and we are all of one blood. Isn't it significant that such a unique service can take place so naturally in a hospital—a house of healing, a place dedicated to helping back to health all men and women no matter what their creed or class or race? This is an unusual congregation and I hope that when you go back to your home church you will remember four of the things that made it so different.

First: You have come because you sincerely desire that your faith in God may be strengthened by this worship experience. You did not dress up to come to this church. You are not here to show off your new hat or your new suit. Nor are you here for social reasons. You have really come to worship. Second: you are here not as a Methodist or a Lutheran or a Catholic. You are here first of all as a child of God. He is your heavenly Father and you have come to worship him in the Spirit of Jesus Christ our Lord. Third: today you are not isolated from your neighbors who have less or more of this world's goods than you, nor are you insulated from those whose skin is of a different color. In this hospital we have one blood bank to take care of all people whatever their race or creed or class, so in this chapel we are all of one family dependent upon the God and Father of us all. And fourth: All of you have been stopped temporarily in your tracks and are now required to spend some time in a hospital bed. This enforced vacation from the frantic pace on the outside has given you the unusual experience of more time to think about those things of spiritual value in your life. As a result you are a very attentive congregation. You tend to participate with your whole being—and this is not always true when you are home and well. It should serve as a reminder to you when you return home of the necessity to stop your frantic pace and see that you regularly take time to strengthen the inner man.

In the hymns and scripture which have preceded these remarks we have declared our dependence upon

God. We have voiced our gratitude to him for his concern for us. We have confessed our own shortcomings and as we hear his word for us, we are reassured of his continued presence with us through the days of the coming week. We ask him that our own weak faith may be stirred up into a living flame. Now that we have again heard his word of reassurance and pardon in the company of other believers we are strengthened in our faith.

As I talk with patients in the hospital, I find that many of you are going through a difficult period these days in relation to your own religious faith. You tell me that you have mixed feelings about your faith. Some of you say in effect, "Chaplain, I am glad that you don't know many of the thoughts which have been going through my mind since I became ill. I thought my faith would be worth something in time of testing but I guess I didn't have very much. I am ashamed of my attitude toward God during these trying days. I have difficulty praying. I have difficulty concentrating on anything and particularly on my faith." This seems to be a prevalent attitude among many patients in the hospital. Illness and sickness can be quite a lonely affair and this is why it can be so helpful for us to gather together with other likeminded people to rekindle the flame that has temporarily gone out within us. Some of you have described your stay in the hospital as a kind of winter period in your life. The nights seem so very long and your spirit is cold and you wonder if spring will ever come again. But every winter happens also to be the time when nature is resting and silently preparing for a new spring. There is every possibility that you will one day look back upon this hospital experience as a creative winter because you temporarily had to lie down in a bed and there was only one place to look and that was up. You found yourself thinking about the vertical dimension in life as you have not had time to think about it while you were running from one task to another outside the hospital.

Now that you have been doing some deeper thinking about your relationship to God, you wish that your faith could do more for you. Of course, being human, you long for a religion that would be easier to follow, easier to understand. You wish that the questions you raise concerning answers to prayer and the presence of God in your life were not as complex as they are. You wish that religion had no mystery. You wish that somehow if you could just believe strongly enough, you could escape from all suffering and uncertainty. In short, what you are really asking is for a religion without a cross. But a religion without a cross would be one that would not meet the demands of the realities of life which each of us has to face. While we may wish that life could be otherwise, life is *not* easy. Life is hard, life is complex, life is a mystery, life is filled with troubles and suffering. But it is because Jesus Christ our Lord also faced the identical kinds of problems which you and I face that we can trust his way of looking at life as making sense even for us.

During this hospital stay many of you will raise questions of a deeper nature than you have raised ever before in your life. As your chaplain I would be more than happy to help you wrestle with some of these problems if you feel that you would like to. I would be most pleased to have the opportunity just to talk informally with you about these matters that are foremost in your mind. In most cases your stay here will be so short that you will not be able to do more than just begin this quest for a deeper understanding of the meaning of your faith, but this is an excellent place in which to make a beginning.

There are growing numbers of patients who come into the hospital for a physical checkup and find that they also are able to have a spiritual checkup at the same time. This checkup often shows that spiritually they are still acting like children who had never gone much beyond a kindergarten understanding of religious matters. Ob-

viously a kindergarten spiritual education is not sufficient
to face the complexities of this modern world where
anxiety and doubt are so predominant. If some of you
are discovering in the midst of suffering that your religious faith is not adequate, perhaps it is because you are
now raising adult questions and the only answers you
have are fit for a child. You are now living in an adult
world and when illness forces you to see the world in all
its stark reality you find that your previous childish ways
of dealing with the issues of life are totally inadequate.

It is our hope that just as everything possible will be
done for you physically and mentally to bring you back
to good working order again, so this experience may
have shaken you out of your spiritual complacency to
think more deeply upon the length and the breadth and
the height and depth of the world in which God has
placed you. Such a quest can be for you a fascinating
adventure as you follow the footsteps of the great men
and women of the Bible who have pioneered for us and
who have passed on their experiences through the written
word in such a way that we no longer need to say that
we are lost in a wilderness of darkness with no light.
The depth of insight of the great prophets of old as they
spoke to the problems of their day are apropos to the
problems of our day. But even more than the prophets
we have Christ our Lord who is the way, the truth, and
the light. He has made it possible for us not to be lost
in a wilderness of darkness and despair. He is the light
which lightens our path. He leads us to fellowship with
our Creator whom he calls "Our Father who art in
heaven." We are grateful for the men and women who
have lived upon this earth before us who have passed
on to us from generation to generation the message of
health, healing, and salvation in Christ which can lead
us to a deep and meaningful relationship even in time
of sickness with our loved ones, with our friends, and
with our God. Amen.

Biographical Sketch

DAYTON G. VAN DEUSEN

Dayton G. Van Deusen was born in the home of a minister, received his A.B. from Hartwick College, his B.D. from Hartwick Seminary and S.T.M. from Union Seminary in New York. He has had clinical training in pastoral care at both general and mental hospitals, has served as the pastor of two Lutheran churches, was for three years a chaplain in the U.S. Army, has served as institutional chaplain for the Nebraska Lutheran Social Service, assistant secretary for chaplaincy services of the National Lutheran Council and is at present Protestant chaplain of the Winneboga State Hospital and staff chaplain of the Lutheran Welfare Services of Wisconsin and Upper Michigan.

His book *Redemptive Counseling* with the subtitle: "Relating Psychotherapy to the Personal Meanings in Redemption" was published in 1960.

He has this to say about a sermon that he prepared for a service of worship in the Leavenworth Penitentiary.

> The principal thoughts resulting in this sermon first began to develop in connection with my work among emotionally disturbed and mentally ill patients. I was struck by several elements in this situation of human suffering: how little, on the whole, these patients thought of themselves and of their possible value; how unacceptable they felt they must be to God and to other persons; how undeserving many of them felt they were of any consideration or mercy or forgiveness. To some extent their sentiments were expressions of three fundamental feelings— worthlessness, badness, and insignificance. In addition there was a rather general feeling of not belonging, of not being wanted.

> The thoughts held by these sick persons contain a great deal of truth about human nature and its frailties. But there is an entire opposite, hopeful, equally factual side of the picture—the aspect presented by the gospel. The gospel does not contradict the dark side of the picture (and of life), but oper-

ates in spite of the dark side and in triumph over
it. This whole saving aspect of the human situation
can easily be ignored and lost sight of in preoccupa-
tion with the more negative aspects. This is what I
felt had been happening in the lives of these disturbed
and ill persons.

Then when the opportunity came to preach in one
of the major penitentiaries of the country, this line
of thought revived. Reflection suggested what earlier
experience with prisoners had already made me feel:
that the same basic factors need to be met and coped
with in the prisoner (rebellious or contrite) as in
the self-depreciating mental patient. Generally the
prisoner is not so openly critical of himself or so
ready to admit needs and failings. Yet underneath
there are the same guilt feelings, the same uncertainty
about himself, and surely the same feeling of not
belonging and of being unwanted. The same hopeful,
saving answers are needed for the prisoner as for
the patient who is in despair or doubt. Therefore,
this sermon was formulated in an effort to counter
some of the defeating and destructive feelings with
elements of a more favorable, truly Christian self-
concept, related to our place in God's redemptive plan.

The direction taken in this sermon is in line with
the goal of pastoral preaching. The relationship of
preaching to pastoral work, for me, centers around
the area of pastoral counseling. The principles and
concepts of pastoral counseling, and its particular
approach to people, are precisely those that will be
involved if preaching is to be pastoral.

The pastoral preacher will respect the personality
and the dignity of each person before him. He will
seek to clarify rather than to impose truth. His message will not be a pronouncement: "Eureka! Here is
what I have discovered!" It will be an invitation:
"Let us search this matter out together." He will see
the truths he speaks about, and will also present or
lead into these truths, in terms of the daily expe-

riences of the persons to whom he is speaking.

The preacher who is truly pastoral will be so familiar with the aspiration and struggle and agonizing of his people that those hearing will know from his preaching, without question, that he understands. Because the tissue of his preaching is the raw material of human nature, he will speak of feelings and dynamics so universal that they are intensely personal to each hearer. And though he deals with such very earthy material, what he says will finally not be sordid because it will be spoken in the transforming light and warmth of the sacrificial love and mercy and redemptive will of God in Christ Jesus. It will bring the hearer together with the ultimate resources of healing and salvation through a deeper and more personal understanding of the gospel.

Sons of God

WHAT WOULD IT BE LIKE to be a son of God? Have you ever been conscious of feeling the way a son of God would feel? It is hard to imagine. We are so aware of feeling like humans that it hardly seems real that we could be such exalted creatures as the term "sons of God" would imply.

Yet the Bible repeatedly says that God intends us to be his sons and that we are, or can be, in this relationship. The Apostle John writes: "Beloved, we are God's children now; it does not yet appear what we shall be, but we know that when he appears we shall be like him, for we shall see him as he is." Think what a value this puts on us. Some of us have already accepted this relationship. But even for those who have not, an enormous value is placed on a person, to have the offer of being his son. God honors us even in the offer.

Other verses and passages also indicate that we are sons of God or eligible to be sons; yet it is most difficult to think so highly of ourselves—that we are of enough value to someone, that someone being God, that he should consider us his sons, or want us to be his sons. Why should it be so difficult to accept God's high evaluation of us? Let us look at some of the things that make us feel as though we are less than he says we are, and compare our feelings with his.

First of all, we are conscious of our own limitations. We know that we are human, and that therefore we have limits to what we can do and be. We come up against a new problem and are aware of our weaknesses in meeting it. We look at our living for the last week and realize many faults. We examine some of our recent decisions and have to raise a question about our judgment. We have obstacles which we are unable to conquer. We find that we are not equal to all of the everyday situations we meet. We all have our inadequacies. And we all have the wrongs and sins in our life of which we are especially conscious. It is little wonder that we are slow to think of ourselves in the class of sons of God.

However, there is more than noting our shortcomings to make us feel too little, too unimportant, and too unworthy to be called God's sons. We are affected by other people's opinions of us and we tend, at least to some extent, to accept these opinions. The result is that we may think less of ourselves than we ought to. Perhaps other persons speak or act as though they do not think we are very important. Maybe the fellows around us start bearing down on us pretty hard and we conclude that they do not like us or think much of us. Or because we have less than other people have, or are less educated, or come from a different background, we may think that they act differently toward us than they should.

We are so made that if someone is angry at us, we may react outwardly in a very forceful and self-assured manner, but we are very likely to raise questions inside about what is wrong with us that made them attack us—and we think less of ourselves. Or if life for some reason doesn't make sense to us, we may conclude that we are not smart enough to see the sense in it, that we are wrong and those who shape our lives are right. Then too, although we know that life has to have some rules and that someone has to administer them, just the fact of having someone over us applying those rules (parents first, others later) makes us feel like small, weak, unimportant creatures. Since we have lived under rules from our earliest days, we may grow up not realizing that we as well as our elders are persons, and that we have a right to ideas of our own, to do some thinking of our own about our living, our standards, our beliefs.

Part of the trouble is that when we were first learning about life, before we could form opinions by ourselves or about ourselves, we had to go by the opinions of others about us—our parents, brothers, or other older people. If we were little or unimportant to them because we were small, we could pick up the idea that we *are* little and unimportant. The saddest thing is that this kind of idea could stay with us even after we are grown, and make us keep on feeling so. Some adults never get over the feeling they picked up as children, that they are less of a person than others around them.

We know, then, that people will not always think as highly of us as we would like. But we do not have to take their opinions of us as true. Most of us can stop and realize that not all people think so poorly of us. We are happy for the number of persons, few or many, who appreciate us and think highly of us—who like us and see value in us, and are ready to be friends because each of us is as significant a person as anyone else.

We should stop and think, at this point, that if other people can make us feel inferior by their attitudes and actions toward us, we can do the same to other persons. We can show the same harmful attitudes toward others and make them feel that they are not worth much because this is the way we treat them. In either case, whether this is done to us or by us, an attitude is shown which does not help us to feel, either about ourselves or others, that we measure up very closely to the name "sons of God."

Thus a knowledge of our own limitations and the opinions of other persons make us rate ourselves lower than God does when he calls us "sons." Another factor that keeps us from boosting our estimation of ourselves any higher is the feeling that we ought to be humble. Humility has been impressed on us as a Christian virtue. Christianity has made an ideal of humility; and the churches, some more than others, have emphasized it. Some insist very strongly that there is no value in us at all, and that this is the only feeling we should ever have about ourselves. They say if God is to be everything, we must be nothing—as if it were necessary to raise God by lowering ourselves! Actually, this emphasis on being humble is only one side of the picture; the Bible teaches us that we *ought* to think something of ourselves. Still this ideal of humility exists, and it is a proper ideal when correctly understood; but it has made us slow to speak highly of ourselves.

We have looked, now, at our opinion of ourselves and at some of the reasons for its being lower than it might be. But what do we find about ourselves if we look at God's relationship to us? Not only can we be, and are we invited to be, his children, but he upholds us and supports us in this position he has decreed for us. Many statements in the Bible reflect this.

". . . You are gods,
    sons of the Most High, all of you.
. . . thou hast made him little less than God,
    and dost crown him with glory and honor.

"See what love the Father has given us, that we should be called children of God."

Even the smallest individual is important to God. Jesus underlined this when he said, "It is not the will of my Father who is in heaven that one of these little ones should perish." Each person is a beloved creature of God, and important to him. It is not enough to say that God has many children and thinks highly of the whole group. This would still not say that one individual was very important; he could be lost in the crowd, indistinguishable from the others. But God's interest is more individual than that.

Some of you have perhaps grown flowers, and know something about how a man grows a new flower. He takes two or more kinds of plant and works with them, using the laws by which things grow—planning, combining, shaping, nourishing—until he comes up with a combination that has never been known before. That flower is important and valuable to the man who developed it. This is just what each of us is to God. We are different from anyone else who was ever made. Each of us is a combination that has never been known before. All of us are important to God, and each one is important.

The emphasis of Jesus on the one sheep that was lost and found, the one sinner who was saved, gives us the key to his own attitude toward people. People to him were individual persons, not just types of one kind or another. When people came to him, or he encountered persons with various sorts of problems, he never put them in categories or mental pigeonholes. He never dealt with people as another case of leprosy, another case of doubt, another case of adultery or bereavement or poverty. In his mind these were persons, each respected as an individual—a person troubled with leprosy, a person troubled with doubt, a person troubled with adultery or bereavement or poverty. We cannot help but think that in his love and respect for persons, Jesus was showing forth the very heart of the way God feels about people.

If we know this, it does not matter so much if some person has a low opinion of us. If he feels that we are of no account, his opinion needs to be compared with God's opinion of us. A family's or a neighbor's unfavorable opinion is not so damaging if we realize that God contradicts it. If someone treats us as inferior, this does not mean that we *are* inferior. If one thinks we are, then he does not understand the whole truth about our value as those whom God has chosen to be his sons.

Let no one think that I am talking now about our being perfect. We are so far from perfect that it is painful. We have our faults and weaknesses; they are many and great. God knows all this about us. The Bible writers know it and speak about our weaker side, as well as our sonship. But the point is that God knows our faults and still calls us "valuable," calls us "sons" or wants us to become his sons. Even our sin and blame do not weaken or remove this offer. If there were anything that would shut us off from him, it would be these—our sins, weaknesses, crimes, selfishness. I do not doubt that everyone, literally everyone, has done things for which he could be imprisoned and punished. Almost everyone, however hardened he may be or however good he may be, sometimes stops and thinks what a poor creature he is, how low, how vile, how ungrateful, how unkind, how far removed from what God wills for him.

Yet in spite of these things that are against us, God accepts us as having worth and value. This is because he loves us. Isn't this the kind of love we have wanted all our lives—the kind of love that doesn't stop when we do something bad, love that does not wither or die when we make mistakes, when we fail to do something to perfection? The father of the prodigal son took him back with all his faults; in the same way God accepts us even with our weaknesses. He wants us to be good, to be creative, to be a credit to him (as far as mere human beings can be); but he remembers that we are made of dust, and he makes allowance for that. He does not expect us to be divine before he will call us his sons. He accepts us for ourselves, because he loves us and wants us—not because of our acceptable behavior, or because of abilities or good looks, or even *because* of being good or holy. He loves us, even while we are imperfect, because we are the persons we are—his chosen children.

Something of the rating God has given us is seen in the place we have in creation. We are the highest part of creation—the only creatures that can have fellowship with God, that can think and decide, can choose the good and try to live by it. He has entrusted creation to us—its care, its development for useful purposes, even the still-unfolding secrets of nature that are now starting to send us unnumbered miles out into space, and providing us with more intense and concentrated power than we ever dreamed was contained in the entire universe. All of this God has entrusted to us.

Another sign of the value God places on people is the fact that he means *us* to treat each other as having worth and value, and has built this principle right into life. Life runs at its best when people treat each other with honor and respect, as we would expect sons of God to be treated. People do misuse each other, but when they do, they endanger their own happiness. Some things cannot be the same when a person has poor relationships with someone else. The feelings of both persons are injured. Any good association they might have had—any business, friendship, cooperative effort, any success or achievement—is affected.

He who treats another poorly suffers in other ways, too. He is at odds with others, perhaps lonely; other people resist him, he is not admitted or accepted into the midst of other people. Or else he suffers inside, is ill at ease with himself, with others, and with God. He who hurts others hurts himself. This is because God has protected our worth by shaping life in such a way that we cannot treat each other as being of little worth, without some unpleasant results. But there is helpfulness and health in seeing another person as a chosen child of God—including the one who does not seem nice or lovable, even the one who has forgotten *our* value and treated us meanly.

God upholds us before other people as his sons, and has made it plain that we do the best thing when we respect the rights and the value of others, when we make allowances for their failings, as he does for ours. This is the principle behind the Golden Rule and the petition in the Lord's Prayer: "Forgive . . . as we forgive."

A final evidence of God's valuing us highly is reflected in what he does within us. He has fitted us wonderfully for the purposes of living here and of growing in our readiness for the life after this one. Besides communing with us and living within us, he has given us remarkable powers for growth, healing, strength, and peace. We may not always be conscious of these powers, but they are there; and if we are ever really motivated to search them out and find them, these powers become more available to us and we may call them forth and use them at times when they are most needed.

If God thinks as much of us as all these evidences make us feel he does, what opinion should we have of ourselves? Should we think more of ourselves than we do? Does this mean that we cannot be humble? Humility need not mean that we are nothing. God created us to be something. When he makes a tree, he expects it to be as much of a tree as it can be. When he makes a useful animal, he expects it to be as much of a useful animal as it can be. And when he makes a man, he wants him to be as much of a man as he can be. Man need not shrink back and say that he is nothing. He is most true to God's wishes and plans when he is as much of a man, and as good a man, as he has it in him to be, and as he can let God make him. He does not have to be cocky and throw his weight around; this is not part of being a man. But

God does allow and wish for man to be something and to consider himself as something of value.

A man can be humble and still be realistic about his assets. Lincoln seems to us like a humble man, but I am sure he knew he was the best rail splitter in the county or the state, and perhaps the ablest lawyer too. It is possible to be humble and still be aware that we can do some certain things better than someone else. A person has a right to self-respect, making the most of himself in a way that is not selfish or arrogant. He has a right to make his own decisions and have his own convictions, which some persons feel too unimportant to do. He has a right to feel that whatever he is, he has a high place in God's estimation and can hold his head up, here on earth, as a worthy person, one whom God has invited into his family as a son.

We see our place, then, in God's thinking. He made us to be his sons, he calls us his loved ones, and he looks to us to accept the relationship of sons. This we do by accepting what God has done for us through his original Son, Jesus Christ. In that event more than in any other way, God showed what a value he places on us, for that main event in the history of creation—the coming of Jesus, his living, loving, serving, suffering, dying, and rising again—was for our sake. This would not have been done for us if we were not dear to God and of great significance to him. Again I must say, this was not done because of our merit but because of his love and therefore our dearness to him. It was necessary for him to do it because our faults and our sinfulness are too much for us. On the one hand, we could not and cannot lift ourselves out of our natural human sinful mess; on the other hand, he in his love could not just leave us in our tragic situation. It was not his nature to look at men and say, "I love them in spite of their sins," and then leave them there in the midst of their predicament. He could not just love us and let us remain vile; he had to do something about our sins. And so he came in Jesus to offer us cleansing and saving and eternal life. This is the greatest token of love anyone has ever known. It is our place to accept what he has done for us who are so important to him, to accept the movement of his love into our lives so that he may cleanse and heal, may save and change us, and may welcome us as sons who have come into the family all the way.

Biographical Sketch

SIGURD D. PETERSEN

ONE OF THE MOST ENCOURAGING SIGNS of our times is the realization that "the retarded can be helped," to borrow a phrase from a pamphlet by Dr. Walter Jacob, pioneer in the work with retarded children. Speaking from the standpoint of the church, it is the realization that the scriptural phrase, "We are the children of God," applies to the retarded as well as to the normal and that the retarded can benefit from a religious ministry. Sigurd D. Petersen condensed this idea into the title of his very helpful book on a religious ministry to the retarded, which he called *Retarded Children: God's Children.* It was a Pastoral Psychology Book Club selection in 1960.

Sigurd D. Petersen is an ordained minister of The American Lutheran Church. In 1929 he graduated from Trinity Lutheran Seminary, now merged with Wartburg Theological Seminary, Dubuque, Iowa. He received his clinical training at the Boys' Industrial School and the Topeka State Hospital, Topeka, Kansas, in 1954-1955. For seven and one-half years he was the Protestant chaplain at the Parsons State Hospital and Training Center, Parsons, Kansas. He has recently returned to the parish ministry at Our Saviour's Lutheran Church, Dannebrog, Nebraska.

He describes the problem of preaching to the retarded as a background for the sermon:

> The Parsons State Hospital and Training Center, located at Parsons, Kansas, is an institution for the mentally retarded with a patient population of 675 from ages six to twenty-one. The mental ability of these children and young people ranges from near zero to dull normal. Of the 600 Protestants approximately 425 attended the two Sunday morning services the years I was chaplain at that institution. The service which they attended was determined by both chronological and mental age.
>
> Preaching to such congregations must of necessity be circumscribed, but it is nevertheless preaching— that is a proclamation of the gospel. The language

used must be as simple as possible and some concepts must be expressed in sentences, or phrases. All ideas expressed and words used should approximate the thought processes of the children which are learned by close association with them.

The message in the sermon ought to be limited to one idea, or impression, and should find expression in concrete life situations. The abstract concepts of our Christian faith such as salvation, redemption, and repentance can be made meaningful not by using such terms, but by conveying assurances and feelings which they bring to the human spirit. The sermon must, therefore, convey a unique quality which can come only from the pastor's own emotional life. If he feels what he says, his audience will, too. This is not accomplished through arm swinging or voice raising. Such techniques are distracting and damaging.

The transfer of feeling of faith, hope, and love is made possible by the retarded's uncanny ability to identify and to be sensitive to a person's moods. Like all others, the retarded reach for that which is pleasing and alleviates stress, so they take to themselves the chaplain's own feelings of assurance and faith.

The effectiveness of preaching Christ, of presenting Jesus to them, becomes apparent. They readily identify with Jesus, his feelings, his love, and his acceptance of people. They see in him what they, perhaps unconsciously, want because of their own needs. This is reason enough for the constant use of gospel lessons or texts. Other Bible characters and texts complicate their problem of dealing with human sin and failures, with which they, too, will identify. To leave them with a sense of guilt and failure is to augment feelings which they already have and with which they are not able to deal. Jesus was always good, he never failed, and his goodness was precisely revealed in his help for the unfortunate and sinful.

I never felt at ease on Sunday morning without a story from the life of Christ. In the religious classes held during the week a teacher could explore what other biblical material could be used advantageously with various groups. The continuous use of texts from the Four Gospels maintained a continuity from week to week and fostered an anticipation for another story about Jesus. Jesus and the people around him became familiar persons. Within this context of a living Savior who not only loved people in bygone days, but who still does, the many aspects of their spirtual needs could be included in an overall preaching program.

In a very definite sense preaching to the retarded, who are confined to an institution, is *pastoral preaching*. Any other type, it seems to me, does not become relevant. To make a "decision for Christ" in the usual meaning of the term or to comprehend exegetical discourses is beyond the ability of these patients. The area of fruitful preaching lies within addressing oneself to their personal needs of which the chaplain becomes quite conscious in his daily contact with them. When he speaks to their feelings of aloneness, separation, sense of uselessness, hopelessness, and anxiety, the chaplain has made contact. When he helps them to identify with Christ and through him to feel the love of God, something important has occurred. Within the confines of God's love, pastoral preaching can begin to structure a meaningful life for the retarded. Because they cannot rationalize life and formulate concepts, their faith, their hope, their love, and their ideals need to be spoken for them. It is not wrong to say to them, "You love Jesus." They will readily indicate, often with an expression of real delight, that this is exactly what they do.

I doubt that the chaplain in an institution for the mentally retarded "writes" his sermons. Most often, as I did, he will use a Bible picture or slide, and then "play it by ear" and react according to the rapport which he has established with his audience. He will come with a well-thought-out message, but he will also be ready to alter his technique or approach. He will not feel frustrated if he must cut his brief sermon short. He will learn to be as spontaneous and unpredictable as his audience, and he will be humbly conscious of the tremendous investment of themselves which retarded children and youth have in their chaplain.

These reflections have in mind preaching to retarded of medium ability. The borderline retardates seem to present a special challenge, if not a problem. The possibility of personal decisions, of rational choices, of spiritual growth would seem to be there. Evidently a number of them lack the mental acumen to become stable personalities. These near-normal individuals, it appears, need considerable structure and guidance toward which they may react negatively. For their own personal growth they need to be confronted with choices and responsibilities, but their responses may be less than what seems reasonable to expect. Perhaps the answer to this problem lies in pastoral counseling with the individual.

The Little Man Jesus Liked

ONE TIME JESUS came to a town called Jericho. Jesus and his friends planned to walk right through the town because they were on their way to Jerusalem. But people wanted to see Jesus, because they liked him, so it was not long before the street was filled with people just as happens in any town when there is a parade. There were so many people that Zacchaeus could not get near to Jesus; and since he was a little man, he could not see Jesus. He could not look over the people because they were taller than he was. So Zacchaeus ran way down the street ahead of the people and climbed up in a tree. There he waited to see Jesus.

Zacchaeus really wanted to see Jesus. He had heard about Jesus. People said that Jesus loved everybody. They said that Jesus helped sick people, that he had just helped a blind man see, and that he told people that he would forgive them when they had sinned. People also said that Jesus would talk to everybody, even to those no one else liked.

How Zacchaeus would like to talk to Jesus! There were not many people who liked Zacchaeus or would talk to him. They thought he was a bad man. They knew that he had taken too much money from people for himself. People really hated Zacchaeus, and perhaps they laughed at him, too, because he was so small. When Zacchaeus thought of Jesus and how Jesus wanted people to live, he was not very happy. He knew he had not always done

168

what was right. Perhaps Jesus could help him in all his trouble so he could be happy.

How was he going to talk to Jesus? Would Jesus see a little man like him? Jesus might think that he was silly sitting up in a tree, and Zacchaeus himself felt a little foolish. In fact Zacchaeus never liked himself. He had always been smaller than other people. When he was a boy, he could not do as much as other boys. He was too small. When he was a young man, he always had to take the back seat, because other young men could push him around. He felt unhappy just as some of you do because you cannot do as much as others. While he sat in the tree waiting for Jesus to come by, he felt sure that Jesus would not care enough even to look at him.

But Jesus did. He looked up and saw Zacchaeus. "Zacchaeus," said Jesus, "come down. I want to go with you to your home." So Zacchaeus came down, and Jesus went with him to his home and talked with him. We do not know what Jesus and Zacchaeus talked about, but Jesus helped him to do what was right. Now Zacchaeus was going to give back the money he had taken from other people. He was going to give much to the poor people who did not have anything. And since he felt that Jesus liked him, it would not bother him any more that he was small. Since Jesus loved him so much that He would not keep thinking about his sins, Zacchaeus knew that the bad things he had done were also forgiven by God. Jesus had said that God was like Him and would not remember the things he had done wrong. Zacchaeus was happy.

Many of us feel like Zacchaeus. Many of us are unhappy because we cannot read or write, or because we are too small, or because we cannot talk very well. We may even feel that we are no good. Maybe we do not like ourselves. We seem alone because we do not have many friends. Like Zacchaeus, we often do wrong to other people because we are unhappy and angry.

Jesus knows all about us. But he loves us anyway. He wants us to remember that he cares about how we feel and what we do. Because Jesus loves us, we love him, and because we know he wants us to do what is right, to be thoughtful and kind to others, we try hard. We can talk to Jesus about all this in our prayers. He understands and he helps.

Biographical Sketch

PAUL MAVES

Congregations in America today have a higher percentage of older persons than did congregations of any previous generation. This will increase, rather than decrease. We mentioned this in an earlier chapter. For this reason, any series of sermons that claims to be pastoral in nature must include an example of preaching that has this problem and this age group in mind.

The man most qualified to make such a presentation is Paul Maves. Dr. Maves has a thorough understanding of both the field of gerontology and of the church. More than any other, he has studied the relationship of the two. In his writing, teaching, and lecturing he has helped many see the significance of the pastoral task with older people and the theological, psychological, and sociological implications of such a ministry.

Dr. Maves has been Professor of Religious Education, Drew University Theological School, Drew University, Madison, New Jersey, since 1949. He was born in Burwell, Nebraska, received his A.B. from Nebraska Wesleyan University, his B.D. from Drew Theological School in 1939, and his Ph.D. from Drew University in 1949. He has also studied at New York University and Harvard University. He has had two quarters of clinical training under the Council for Clinical Training of Theological Students and has held pastorates in Nebraska, New Jersey, New York, and Vermont. He was ordained an elder of the Methodist Church in 1940. He is a member of Troy Annual Conference of the Methodist Church. Dr. Maves served with the Department of Pastoral Services of the Federal Council of Churches of Christ from 1946 to 1949, for two years as research associate and one year as acting executive secretary. He is co-author with J. Lennart Cedarleaf of *Older People and the Church;* editor of *The Church and Mental Health;* author of *The Best Is Yet to Be* and *Understanding Ourselves as Adults,* and contributor to journals and symposia.

He provides us with a description of the setting and the purposes of the sermon which follows:

> This sermon was prepared as an address to be given at the closing banquet of a national conference on the Ministry to the Aging held by the Mennonite Church at Goshen, Indiana, on November 1, 1961. A number of senior citizens over eighty years of age were the guests of honor on this occasion. Therefore this sermon posed the double task of helping church officials think about the meaning of the church's ministry to the aging and to confirm for the aged in the group their assured place and role in the church. The uniting idea was that this ministry belonged to the older as well as to the younger, and involved not only being ministered to but also ministering to others.
>
> I have found in my experience in talking about aging to older people that they respond to an open facing and frank discussion of its meanings, whatever they may be. Basically the problem of aging is the universal problem of facing change and loss as well as the pain which may be experienced as a result. Furthermore, it is a process in which we are all existentially involved as it affects us and our relations to others.
>
> Perhaps there are those who would not classify this as a sermon at all, since it is so didactic. Yet I believe it is, for it does affirm what God has done for us in Christ and it is an exposition of what his mighty acts mean for us in a concrete relationship.
>
> It is addressed to those who have already heard the gospel and who believe it. Therefore all that is needed is to remind them of the gospel they have received and to plunge into the question of what this now means for us in specific terms. If the congregation had included numbers of persons to whom the

gospel had not been proclaimed or who had not really listened, more time would have to be spent on the Kerygma. In this case, such a sermon would have been preached within the context of a program of preaching which would have laid the groundwork for it.

Senior Citizens
and the Household of God

BEFORE WE CAN GO FAR in talking about the ministry of the church to older people, we must talk about the nature and the purpose of the church and of its ministry. This is important because many persons have a distorted notion of what the church is and does. Some think of it as a building which stands in a particular place or as what takes place within that building. From this point of view a church is what we go to. Some think of it as an organization something like a social club or a service club made up of persons who like each other and want to work together to achieve common purposes. From this point of view a church is what we join. Others think of the church as a kind of service agency for persons in trouble who attend the service of worship or consult the pastor whenever they have a sense of personal need. From this point of view the church is what we use.

From the point of view of the scriptures, however, the church is basically a community of persons. The church is to be found wherever these persons are, whether gathered in one place for a meeting or scattered at work and play. It is the community of those who have been touched and transformed by the love of God which was in Christ, who have been received into this community, and who are growing up into the maturity which was in him. It is the community in which Jesus is acknowledged as the Christ and as Lord. Because its members have experienced and are now experiencing the love of God, they are being remade. They are different because they see

174

things through new eyes, they weigh things with a different set of scales. They have in them the mind of Christ. From this point of view the church is a people of whom the individual becomes a part.

The church is made up of those whom God has called out of the world to come into fellowship with Christ and who have responded to the call. This call is to every person regardless of age. God is no respecter of persons. He does not pay much attention to the distinctions we like to draw. He is not taken in by the masks we wear. Among the pilgrim people of God no one is excluded because he is old nor is he valued less because his hair is gray.

The church is still more than this. The church is a royal priesthood. Persons are called out of the world in order to be fitted to go back into the world as ministers of Christ. The church does not exist for itself but for the world, which God so loved that he gave his only begotten Son that whosoever believes in him might have eternal life. Every Christian is a minister. To become one of God's people is not to seek asylum but to join an arduous rescue operation. The Lord's Supper is not a banquet for those who have arrived, but a picnic lunch for an army on the march. Every Christian is a minister.

This is our calling: to serve God wherever we are in whatever we do. In this ministry the unordained laity has a crucial part, for it is they who come into touch with the world. They are the ones who carry the gospel into the market place, into the halls of learning, into the factories, and out on the farms. When the church is gathered for worship, the clergy is the chief minister and the laymen are his assistants. But when the church is scattered abroad the laymen are the chief ministers and the clergymen are their assistants.

Just as every Christian is a minister, and just as he has been called regardless of his educational attainments or his intelligence quotient or his ability to make speeches or his social standing, or his physical vigor, even so there is no retirement from this ministry because of age. The nature of his ministry may change as capacities and opportunities change, but he continues to serve God as long as he draws breath. Even the person who is completely dependent upon others for physical care has a call to minister. It may be his vocation to witness to the love of God to those who care for him. The hospital room may be his parish.

I once knew an elderly woman who for many years was bent and twisted by arthritis. She spent her days in a wheel chair, for she had only the use of a few fingers and slight movements of the arms. Every one of these movements caused pain. I was designated as her pastor, but I never came to call without feeling that it was I who was ministered to, and I always left both humbled and inspired by the way she served her Lord with radiance and faith. She loved the church and she liked to keep in touch with its programs. She read everything the church could send her. She liked to have company. She had a telephone beside her chair and with it she kept a card file of birthdays and anniversaries of a long list of persons. Every day she called those whose birthday or wedding anniversary it was, to wish them well. She used some of her time to crochet exquisite lace for the annual bazaar the women of the church held, and people were glad to buy it not only because it was beautiful but also because of what it represented.

This ministry of the church in which all of us share, regardless of age, is the expression of our love for Christ, our response to what God has done for us in creating us, preserving us, and redeeming us. Our ministry is our way of saying, "Thank you." Because God loved us we cannot but love others, knowing that Christ died for them also. We cannot love God and hate or belittle our brother.

Our ministry is worship. Our worship takes three forms. We worship God with the words we speak or write. Sometimes these words are addressed to God as others listen. Sometimes they are addressed to other persons, knowing that God is listening. They may be words of prayer and praise. They may be words of encouragement and admonition. They may be words of testimony in which we recite what God has done for us.

We worship God with the deeds we do. Some of these deeds are dramatic or symbolic acts, as when we bow in prayer or participate in the sacraments. Sometimes they take the form of kindly acts, as when we give a cup of cold water to the thirsty man or pay a visit to those who are shut in. Carrying a casserole to a bereaved neighbor, smoothing the pillow of a sick patient, or processing the application for admission to a home for the aged can be sacraments if done with love in the name of Christ and if received in faith. These sacramental acts may either convert the unbeliever to Christ or nurture the Christian in his faith.

We worship God through the fellowship we have with one another. What we are and how we relate to others may be a telling witness to the transforming power of God's love. The people in the early days of the church said in wonder, "Behold these Christians, how they love one another!" and this love drew persons to Christianity. The attitudes we take toward persons and the way we treat them may speak louder than all we say with our mouths. Professor Abraham Heschel said at the White House Conference on Aging that a culture was to be tested not by its scientific achievements nor by its power to produce consumer goods, but by its reverence, its humaneness, its compassion, and its sense of justice. The test of a religious people is the attitude it takes toward the aged. It is easy to love children. Even the dictators make a display of loving children. Even the lower animals seem to have something of a mothering instinct which leads them to care for the young. But only man undertakes to care for the aged.

Elton Trueblood has suggested that perhaps the real test of the church's claim to be a community that is sincerely committed to love of God and neighbor is whether or not any member could be assured that if anything happened to him and his wife, the congregation would assume responsibility for his children. Doubtless he would include in this the care of an aged father or mother.

Leo Simmons, an anthropologist who has studied aging in many societies around the world, has written that:

Nature in the raw has never been very kind to old age in any species. The cycle of life begins and ends under conditions of dependency; but in the end stages of dependency there are apparently no 'instincts' or inborn propensities which impel the offspring to sustain the ancestor that matches or compares with the biologically determined 'parental drives.' . . .

Everywhere the human cycle also begins with the dependency of the young on those who are older, and, unless it is cut off early, it ends with the dependency of the old on those who are younger . . . (However, we do find that man can) learn, be taught, inspired, or impelled to respect, succor, and sustain his grandparents.[1]

Thus old age is distinctly a human-cultural achievement. Some cultures and some societies have provided the security to make successful old age possible. It must be permitted by the environment. It must be supported and sustained by the culture. A mutually supportive relationship between the youth and their elders must be established, in which there is loving and being loved. The benefits of the care of the aged must be seen by the

[1] From "Aging in Preindustrial Societies," by Leo Simmons in *Handbook of Social Gerontology: Societal Aspects of Aging*, edited by Clark Tibbitts (Chicago: University of Chicago Press, 1960), p. 64.

younger. The assumption of responsibility for the care of the aged must be based upon affection.

So it is that in the scriptures we read, "Honor your father and your mother, that your days may be long in the land." It is religious faith in the Judeo-Christian tradition which assigns value to persons as persons because they are created in God's image and called to be his children. It is this faith which recognizes the centrality of a mutually supportive love and affection between persons in the kingdom of God. That people is strong in which each group believes that it has a secure place at each stage of existence. Fundamentally, the concern for the weak and the aged is a product of religious faith.

Let us think more specifically about the strategy of our ministry with reference to the senior citizens among the people of God. And let me repeat that this is more than the ministry of the ordained clergy. No minister, regardless of how brilliant, how well trained, or how conscientious, can do all the ministering that needs to be done. We cannot move the church forward by simply adding new programs and new duties to the clergyman's job description. The ministry of the church to this group of persons that is emerging in our society with increasing significance is a ministry of the whole church.

It is a ministry which has good news and a message of reconciliation for the aging. The aging include those who have reached and passed the age of retirement, those who are becoming aware of declining energy and of approaching retirement, those who are looking ahead and making plans for the mature years, the last one fourth of their life. A ministry to and with and by the aging includes all of us. Each of us is aging. Each of us faces change and the challenge to adjust to change. This is a ministry which unashamedly seeks to meet human needs where it finds them, whether these be physical needs for food, clothing, shelter, and medical care, or spiritual needs such as affection, self-respect, and a sense of significance among the family of man.

This is a ministry which says to the aging: "You are created in the image of God. Christ died for you. God loves you in spite of mistakes, failures, weaknesses, lack of social status, or increasing disability. God loves you for yourself and not for what you can produce or give to others, or for the recognition you have achieved, or for the power you possess. You do not need to try to justify yourself and your existence in his sight by working, by being useful, or by producing. Give up the attempt to earn the love of others by your good works, by giving gifts, or by leaving an estate. Accept the love which is offered you, and walk with Christ wherever he leads you. Let what you do be out of gratitude and not out of fear."

Social security and material comfort are important, but they do not matter ultimately. If we really believe this, we can use what we have as instruments of our love. We might even pay our taxes cheerfully to the extent that they go to meet human need. The church gives physical care to needy persons because it loves them. But it gives more. It gives care with warmth, affection, and respect. Ultimately what is important is the quality of the relationship which is expressed in the way adequate care is given.

To the aging the church will say: "Aging is a natural process which is a part of the plan of God. Aging is not to be confused with disease. Disease is a departure from the plan of creation, but aging is in accordance with the plan. God sees it as good. The death of the physical body is a part of his plan also and need not be feared, for nothing can separate us from his love. We do not know what we shall be when physical death comes, but we know that it will be good, for he has contrived it. The death we fear and which comes from sin is the death of the spirit. We can have true life. Eternal life is a quality of existence that is available to us here and now in the midst of the pain and travail of our living. The kingdom of God has come. We have a foretaste here of the glory that is to be."

To the aging the church will say: "God has given you gifts. Each new day, each encounter is a gift. You have capacities and talents. You are rich in experience, in memory, in perspective. You are to be responsible stewards of his gifts. Find yourself by losing yourself, by giving yourself away in his service. Come and follow him. Spend the day joyfully in his ministry. Participate in his work where you find yourself. 'The chief end of man is to glorify God and to enjoy him forever.' Herein lies your significance and fulfillment."

If we believe that, we will practice vocational counseling to help the aging know their gifts and find areas of service. We will try to open doors which will enable them to use and not to bury their gifts. The aged should not kill time, but should redeem it through worship and work within the range of their capabilities. Our goal in this area of vocational counseling is, wherever possible, the conservation of the ability to function which older persons possess, rehabilitation of capacities needlessly lost, and then constructive investment of these capabilities.

The church not only ministers to the aging, but it calls them to participate in its ministry—its mutual ministry within the people of God, its mutual ministry to the world. There are many ways this ministry may be fulfilled. There are many roles through which the ministry goes forward. It is these roles which lend significance to life, which structure their time, and which enable them to find meaning in their existence.

Let us, then, think about the various roles which older people can take in the ministry of the people of God, and of what the church can do to enable them to take these roles with satisfaction to themselves, as well as for God's glory.

First, there is the role of the worshiper—he who listens to God's word, confesses his faith, and renews his commitment. It is important that the hearing of the word be done in the congregation, for God speaks through persons and personal relationships. Older people need the opportunity to participate in corporate worship. Unfortunately, older people drop out of participation because of increasing physical disability, lack of transportation facilities, and often lack of financial resources. Then, too, loss of a spouse, moving to a new community, and a feeling of not being particularly welcome or wanted discourage participation. The church needs to consider ways of making it possible for persons to participate in worship. Transportation pools, neighborhood meetings, televised and recorded services, and services in the home may be helpful. Hearing aids, elevators, hymnals with large type often make the difference between ability and inability to participate. A personal visit and a warm welcome may provide the extra incentive to make the effort to participate.

Second, there is the role of witness, or bearer of the word. Many older people can serve as teachers, advisers, and friendly counselors. Their testimony to the meaning of faith may inspire a congregation. Their reflection upon history may illuminate the present. Children and youth who do not have the opportunity to know attractive older people are impoverished in their experience.

Third, there is the role of pastor, or one who is responsible for the spiritual nurturing and care of others. Older people often find significant service as friendly visitors and pastoral callers. Sometimes they can participate by being part of a telephone chain. Sometimes a link may be forged between an older person and a young person who may need a grandparent, to the benefit of both. They may participate in intercessory prayer for those in need.

Fourth, there is the role of a servant, which is the one our Lord chose for himself. This is to be a deacon in the house of the Lord, doing those things which need to be done but which are too often treated as if they were trivial because they must be done behind the scenes. The occupational skills of the retired may be contributed to the church. A carpenter can repair broken chairs, a plumber can fix leaky pipes, an accountant can help keep the records. Others can address letters, serve as stewards of equipment, act as hosts or hostesses at reception desks or on welcoming committees. Sometimes work can be designed to fit the capacities of the worker more easily than workers can be found to fit the jobs as we usually describe them.

Fifth, there is the role of elder, or designated leader. One should be selected to serve because he can and because he is best fitted, not because of his age. It is not good if the elderly hold all the positions of leadership. It is tragic if those who are older are not training others to take their places. Many of the senior citizens may feel they have fulfilled their obligation and have earned the right to be relieved of arduous and demanding responsibilities. But certainly the senior citizens need to be allowed to speak up for themselves, and they have a right to be heard as much as any other group. In the church there may be a decade after retirement when a senior citizen has the vigor as well as the time to put his considerable experience at the disposal of his church. With the trend toward earlier retirement there will be even more time. More and more we are hearing of older people who, having raised their families and having provided for their retirement, are selling their business or quitting their job to engage in some kind of service in the needy places of the world.

Paul had to write to Timothy: "Let no one despise your youth, but set the believers an example. . . . Do not neglect the gift you have, which was given you by prophetic utterance when the elders laid their hands upon you . . . by so doing you will save both yourself and your hearers."—1 Timothy 4:12, 14, 16

The time may be at hand when we shall have to say to the senior citizens among the people of God: "Let no one look down upon you because of your age, but set the believers an example. . . . Do not neglect the gift you have which is given you as an elder. You have a responsibility to make of life a song of praise and a light along the highway of God. Serve faithfully in the household of God all your days. In so doing you will save both yourself and those who listen to you."

Biographical Sketch

JOHN CHARLES WYNN

Wide attention is being given families and their problems in current American life. Family experiences loom steadily more significant for personal development and social welfare. There has been an alarmingly high percentage of family failure. There is almost universal agreement among those who study families that most of their problems and needs are spiritual. Family-serving social agencies, medical and psychiatric specialists—as well as religious leaders—concur in this judgment.[1]

This statement was written by Richard E. Lentz, in the introduction to a book *Sermons on Marriage and Family Life,* edited by John Charles Wynn. Then he went on to point out the need for Christian preachers to "challenge, comfort and guide families in the complex situations of modern life."[1]

No one is more qualified for such a task than John Charles Wynn, Professor of Religious Education at the Colgate-Rochester Divinity School. Few men have had as wide a range of experience in the field of the church and family life as he. He did his undergraduate work at College of Wooster and his theological training at Yale University. Throughout his career he has specialized in family life education and the church. He has had experience in the local church, serving Presbyterian churches in Evanston, Illinois, and El Dorado, Kansas. He has served as Director of Family Education Research for the United Presbyterian Board of Education. He attended the study conference on "The Church and Marriage," at Celigny, Switzerland, and traveled throughout Europe studying centers where churches were engaged in family education. He has served as chairman of the National Council of Churches Department of Family Life; he is a member of the National Council of Family Relations, the National Association of Marriage Counselors, and the National Advisory Committee of Clergymen of the Planned Parenthood Federation of America. He is on the Board of Directors of the National Family Life Foundation and serves on the Casework Committee of the Family Service Association of Rochester.

[1]*Sermons on Marriage and Family Life,* John C. Wynn, ed. (Nashville: Abingdon Press, 1956), p. 7.

He has published two books in the general area of family life and the church: *A Pastoral Ministry to Families* and *How Christians Face Family Problems.* He edited a book of *Sermons on Marriage and Family Life,* and was co-author, with Roy Fairchild, of a significant research project, *"Families in the Church: a Protestant Survey."* He has also contributed chapters to numerous volumes on family life and has written many articles in this same field.

A quotation from one of these books gives an introduction to his thought about preaching on the family and the home. In a section in which he outlines the various types of worship services that are possible for families, and the wide variety of topics that are available, he says:

. . . Instruction does play a part in preaching; but that is not preaching's primary purpose. The real concern of preaching is to proclaim God's Word with all of its good news: that God is reconciling the world unto himself, that with him there is forgiveness of sin. The preacher who sees his task in this light will not seek by any superior-to-thee pulpit stance to tell his pewholders how to have an upright family (they may just be doing a better job of it than the cleric), but rather will do something far more important by relating the good news of God to family living. . . . In this approach is a healthy recognition that we have not surmounted all our problems, and that we share with our people the need for God's grace in family living.[2]

---

[2]From *Pastoral Ministry to Families* by John Charles Wynn. Copyright 1957, W. L. Jenkins. The Westminster Press. Used by permission.

The Family of God

*While he was still speaking to the people, behold,
his mother and his brothers stood outside, asking
to speak to him. But he replied to the man who
told him, "Who is my mother, and who are my
brothers?" And stretching out his hand toward
his disciples, he said, "Here are my mother and
my brothers! For whoever does the will of my
Father in heaven is my brother, and sister, and
mother."*

—Matthew 12:46-50

To THAT VAST PORTION of American public sentiment for
which family life may be described only in terms of the
ideal, it must seem unusually jarring to read of some of
the family relations of Jesus. The quality of home life
cherished in our often-discussed concept of togetherness
is challenged by several of the teachings of Jesus. Prominent among these is an incident that occurred in Galilee.

To reconstruct that scene, we can imagine his teaching
one of the sizable crowds that had begun to gather
around him wherever his Galilean tour took shape. In the
midst of his session with the people, some man, unnamed
in the Scripture but probably one of the disciples, tact-
fully interrupted him. Speaking quietly to him, he indicated that Mary and her sons had arrived from Nazareth
and were on the outskirts of the crowd with a message
for him. It is not difficult to conjecture what that message
would have been, had it been delivered. Not a few of the
folks in Nazareth, who must have included some friends
and relatives, had come to consider Jesus quite beside
himself. This unexpected turn of events that had taken
one of their number on a traveling ministry of healing
and teaching was too unconventional for them to accept.
Very likely Mary and her sons had come to persuade Jesus to return home with them to a more normal village
life.

Jesus was heedless to this tender trap, and declined the invitation with memorable words. With a gesture of mingled love and desperation, he indicated those about him and exclaimed, "Here are my mother and my brothers." He was pointing to his disciples.

This so often is the way of Jesus. He is a never-ceasing surprise to us, stern where we might expect him to have been tender, gentle where we might have supposed him to become harsh. This surely can be classified as one of his harder sayings about people. Still it is one with other words of similar stripe: "He who loves father or mother more than me is not worthy of me," or "A man's foes will be those of his own household." These strike a dischordant note into our contemporary mellowness about family life unless we study its context carefully.

II

If we face up to biblical facts, we must note that Jesus had been rather independent of his family ties for some time. Not only had his infancy been attended by grim prophecy ("a sword will pierce through your own soul," Simeon had told Mary), but the only glimpse that we get of his childhood shows him to have been a precociously autonomous personality. Then when he had grown up, instead of assuming traditional Jewish family roles of marriage, family, and a trade, he entered a teaching ministry to the dismay of folks in his home town. Indeed, when afterward he revisited Nazareth, it was to be rebuffed and misunderstood so that here, of all places, he could accomplish no mighty works. Now ironically it was to this same Nazareth that his mother and brothers wanted him to return. But to what? To a town that had rejected him—that had very nearly lynched him by mob violence when he offended them in their synagogue. "He came to his own home, and his own people received him not." The

Gospel puts it plainly: his own brothers did not believe in him.

If strains sometimes showed through his family relations, Jesus could apply the memory of them to his teachings about other families. He was able to refer aptly to the rivalry of brothers, to the patience of a father who daily scans the horizon to see if his absent son might return, or to the breaking point of a marriage as "your hardness of heart." Nor was that all. He was apt to phrase his profoundest teachings in family terms. His hearers were a people of close-knit family ties; and for all their home problems evidenced in New Testament references, they valued their family life highly. With real empathy they understood parables and allusions that featured a householder who would not arise at night for his neighbor's plea, lest he waken his sleeping children who were hard to get to sleep again after a midnight arousal. They knew intimately what he meant when he alluded to the labor pains of a woman in childbirth, to a mother weeping for her children, to a landowner who entrusted a difficult mission to his own son.

Such references enabled them to understand what he was getting at that day when he indicated that his disciples were his real family. They realized that this larger family was marvelously accepting, yet sternly demanding. It was to take precedence over other claims; they were first to seek this new household and only later to add other things. When one would-be disciple requested extra time to fulfill final obligations to his aged father, our Lord replied directly: "Leave the dead to bury their own dead." That James and John understood this is seen in the history of their call. When Jesus summoned them, they immediately abandoned their nets and apparently left their thunderous father, Zebedee, standing dumbstruck in his boat, and followed him. Thus it was that some members of his new family were able to compre-

hend that God is a father who is not only more merciful
and loving than any earthly father can be, but also more
demanding.

Indeed, it was possible to illustrate the goodness of
God by comparing him to ordinary fathers like ours: "If
you then, . . . know how to give good gifts to your children, how much more will your Father who is in heaven
give good things to those who ask him?" Such sayings
were meaningful only because both Jesus and his hearers
had so deep a regard for family life. When he insisted
that the requirements for discipleship transcend family
loyalty, he was saying in effect that such discipleship is
so important that it outweighs even the dearest and finest
of earthly ties, even the family.

III

Such a scripture passage then serves as a sober corrective to the vast sentimentalism that surrounds much of
American family life today. The sociologist identifies this
phenomenon within "neo-familism"; and the advertiser
identifies it succinctly as "togetherness." Whatever our
term, it is instructive to see that the life and teachings of
Jesus cannot be cited in unmixed support for family sentimentality. That which we have been witnessing in recent
years may go well beyond mere sentimentality to sheer
idolatry, as we have sometimes tended to treat the home
as a veritable god of sorts. We need to review that which
Paul Tillich has emphasized: "The family is no ultimate."[3]
And indeed, it is not; for God is our Ultimate. "You shall
have no other gods (no, not even this one) before me."

In a survey with which I was connected a couple of
years ago, we interviewed hundreds of church families

---

[3] See Paul Tillich, *The New Being* (New York: Charles Scribner's Sons, 1955),
pp. 105ff.

all across the nation. Over and again they stressed the fact that they valued their times together, but they also cherished times they could be freed from each other's company, to be spared from too much togetherness.⁴ In this admission there is nothing shameful or sinful. We are all so constructed that we need to get away from family ties. This, in fact, is an actual developmental task of the adolescent. His is a period of turbulence and strain as he works through his new role, and prepares by stretching his independence to become emancipated into manhood. It happens that in our social system we know this emancipation to be essential. Our teen-agers must grow, must become mature adults, must venture forth on their own. Not to do so can be tragic. Psychologists teach us that our very mental health requires such a maturing process. There are few sadder sights than that of a grown man who is still tied to the apron strings of his parents. Many a drama depicts this as a tragedy, e.g. *The Silver Cord, Look Homeward, Angel,* and *The Death of a Salesman.* These, among others, show dramatically what case histories demonstrate clinically, namely that prolonged dependence upon the family can become unhealthy.

It may be consoling, but perhaps only dismaying, to note that rebelliousness in an adolescent sometimes arises precisely because parents have done a good job in rearing their children. Thus to have freed young people may be at times painful even while it is wise. Paradoxically there are times when parents must show their love by ceasing to grasp the object of their loving, viz., their sons and daughters. It is important for us to know that the home, no less than Cape Canaveral, can be a launching pad. From it our young people go out into their autonomous life and into maturity.

---

⁴See Roy W. Fairchild and J. C. Wynn, *Families in the Church: a Protestant Survey* (New York: Association Press, 1961).

IV

Christians of the early church knew what it means to become independent of their family because there were times when they were disowned by their families for following Christ. A similar experience may happen today to the Moslem who is converted to Christianity, to an East German, or in some cases to an American. Yet it is possible for them to find a new family fellowship in the church. Jesus included his followers in his new concept of the family of God. Paul was to take up this concept in his term "the household of God," and in a different connection, "the church in your house."

In significant ways the early church was a family. They shared their bread, their resources, their spiritual sustenance as they found themselves with new brothers and sisters in the faith. The church has become the family of God; and everyone in it is mother, or brother, or sister to every one else in it because each is first of all a mother, or brother, or sister in Christ. Make no mistake about it: we are all related to each other through him, whether we would have chosen to be or not.

It may be difficult for the average church member to imagine that the church family could ever replace his own family for him. If so, it may be because he has come from a loving home. There are others, however, who know at first hand what hate, and misery, and loneliness can be present in some families. Everyone knows of broken marriages that have featured vindictiveness. Everyone knows cases of unworthy parents who mistreat, neglect, or abandon their own children. It is the realization of such grim factors that makes the blind glorification of parenthood or the idolatory of family life so ludicrous. Truly we are always on unsteady footing when we glorify mere persons.

Somehow this large family under the fatherhood of God has a depth of dependability that no earthly family ever quite attains.

> For my father and my mother have forsaken me,
>   but the LORD will take me up

asserts the psalmist. The family of God has within it a love that will not let us go because it is infinite love. It carries with it the redemptive forgiveness of a loving father who puts up with our adolescent rebelliousness against him (a state the theologian labels as sin) and, allowing us our freedom, yet follows us with his mercy.

When, therefore, Jesus stretched out his hand to his followers and said, in effect, "These are my family," he was not so much rejecting his own mother and siblings as he was including them in the larger family of God. He was not inviting us to love our kinfolk less so that we could love ourselves more. He was opening to us his Father's house where we are all at home. He was gathering us into a family replete with its terrible demands upon us, upon our faith, and upon our loyalties, yet also with its wonderful inclusiveness of every last one of us, no matter how low we have come or how unworthy we may be. That is some small hint of what we mean when we speak of the grace of God.

PART III

Fulfill Your Ministry

Sermons preached to theological students and pastors

And he said to them, "The kings of the Gentiles
exercise lordship over them; and those in
authority over them are called benefactors. But
not so with you; rather let the greatest among
you become as the youngest, and the leader
as one who serves."

—Luke 22:25-26

"As the Father has sent me, even so I send you."

—John 20:21

Of this gospel I was made a minister according
to the gift of God's grace which was given
me by the working of his power.

—Ephesians 3:7

". . . fulfil your ministry."

—2 Timothy 4:5

The word minister means "to serve." As D. T. Niles has pointed out in his thought-provoking little book, *The Preacher's Calling to Be Servant*, "we are preachers not because God has called us to be preachers but because God has called us to be servants. When we surrendered ourselves to Him, we surrendered ourselves to become His servants." This concept includes both preaching and pastoral care. To quote Niles further, "It is not merely to the service of preaching that one is called, but rather to be servant to those to whom one preaches," and again "however true one's message may be it needs to be rooted in a servant's life."[1] If one is to be true to such a demand, if one is to "fulfill" such a ministry, he too needs to have his own faith strengthened, his vision constantly renewed. We have included two sermons in this series which were prepared with the minister himself in mind. One was prepared for theological students as they completed their training and moved to positions of greater responsibility; the other was prepared for pastors in the field. As the pastor constantly preaches in order that his people may attain maturity in the faith, so he needs guidance and strength in order that he may fulfill his ministry.

---

[1] pp. 44, 52, 58.

Biographical Sketch

Daniel Day Williams, in his book, *The Minister and the Care of Souls,* includes an interesting chapter entitled, "The Minister's Self-Knowledge." In it he states, "Those who undertake the care of souls must attain self-understanding."[1] The pastor must understand himself and he must understand the ministry. It was felt that a series of sermons like this should include one prepared with theological students in mind.

Dr. Williams, because of his background of practical experience and thorough scholarship, is unusually well qualified to speak to the needs of the young minister. He is Professor of Systematic Theology at Union Theological Seminary, in New York. For many years he was a member of the faculty of the Chicago Theological Seminary. Prior to that time he served in the parish ministry, as pastor of the First Congregational Church, Colorado Springs, Colorado. He received his education at Denver University (A.B.), University of Chicago (A.M.), Chicago Theological School (B.D.), and Columbia University (Ph.D.).

He is recognized as one of the leading theologians of our day, and has been invited to give the Rauschenbusch Lectures at Colgate-Rochester Divinity School, the Nathaniel Taylor Lectures at Yale, the Earl Lectures at Pacific School of Religion, and many others.

He is the author of three significant volumes: *God's Grace and Man's Hope; What Present-day Theologians Are Thinking; The Minister and the Care of Souls.*

He describes the occasion and the background of this sermon as follows:

> This sermon was addressed to a graduating class of theological students. The topic arose out of discussion with the students themselves. The sermon was addressed to a real concern of future ministers. There are of course aspects of the ministry and the Christian life which have special pertinence to theological students, and these need not be excluded in preaching to

[1] Williams, *The Minister and the Care of Souls* (New York: Harper & Row, Publishers, Inc., 1961), p. 95.

197

them. Ministers do have some special problems. At the same time every important aspect of the Christian life bears upon the life of the whole church and of all men. In preaching to theological students in relation to their special tasks, there can be the continual reminder that it is the life of the whole church which is our final concern, not the problems of any one group within the church.

Authority and Ministry

MANY OF YOU WHO GRADUATE TONIGHT entered Union
Seminary, as I did, three years ago. For some it has been
a shorter or longer period. In these years we have worked,
studied, and worshiped together. We have criticized one
another, and encouraged one another. Now you go to
every part of the world: to churches, to schools, and to
mission fields. Many go to be pastors, and, in the spirit
of an eighteenth-century church rule, "to preach the word
of God publicly, purely, briefly, clearly, thoroughly, and
to edification." Others are to be teachers, church musicians, chaplains, and counselors. Most of us on the faculty, after due consideration, have elected to remain
behind. There are a few more books to read, classes to
teach, elusive ideas to clarify. . . .

I

If we think of the questions which have been most
discussed among us in these past years here in this school,
we might agree that they have revolved around the two
poles of "Authority" and "Ministry"; and more especially
around the specific question of the authority by which
we minister in the church. By what right do we offer
ourselves as preachers and teachers, not just of our own
words, but of the Word of God? We will find some of
our congregation standing in awe of the office of the ministry and of us within it. We will find others who stand
in no awe of us whatsoever, and who are waiting to be
shown with what authority we speak.

What gives this question of authority its intensity is the suspicion that much of what passes for authority in religion today is but the echo of our own human voices. We see a clear issue between a trust in human judgment and ideals, and a trust in the divine truth which judges and corrects our human thoughts and ways. Amidst the clamor of many voices we are seeking that absolute righteousness which is God's own truth setting us straight. The world is full of authorities: political, legal, moral, and scientific. And we often hear it said that "the authorities disagree." That is a revealing phrase about all earthly authority. But we are ministers speaking of Him who is the author of our salvation. How is this possible for us fallible human beings? No wonder P. T. Forsythe says, "The question of authority in its religious form is the first and last issue of life."

II

There are many points to be made about the evangelical view of authority; but I wish to call our attention to just one consideration which bears especially upon the work of the Christian minister, though we shall not forget that every Christian is a minister in the name of Christ.

The point is this: the truth which God reveals and which we are to preach and teach is one which comes in the midst of the struggles and perplexities of life. God speaks in such a way that we are bound to accept the trial and error, the searching and the suffering of human life if we are to hear and proclaim his authoritative word. Such authority as belongs to us is that which comes only as we participate in the spirit of Christ's ministry to human life, and that means his service in the midst of human problems.

This way of looking at the meaning of authority finds its justification in the way the Bible speaks of God's revelation to men.

The prophets indicated the word of God "thus saith the LORD." But the prophets were men who listened for the word of God by a constant attention to the life of their people. They looked into the faces of the hungry, the angry, the faithless. They saw the pride of nations and the hopes of the oppressed. And they risked seeing their specific judgments and predictions corrected by history. Who would say that even the greatest prophets were always right in their predictions of what God would do? They pointed to the righteousness of God which was present, yet moving in mysterious ways.

Even more clearly, the New Testament shows that the Word of God comes only through a man's bearing with the human perplexity and groping. What is it in the New Testament account of Jesus of Nazareth which is supremely authoritative? That indeed is not a simple question. There is a magisterial power in the figure of Jesus. He spoke as one having authority and not as the scribes. He commanded the demons and went about healing. He called upon men who are weary and heavy laden to come and follow him, for his yoke is easy and his burden light. But when he came into conflict with the authorities, when he met the resistance of men to the message of the kingdom, the son of God did not brush aside the obstacles with a gesture of omnipotence. He had to go through them, and to share our human limitations and estrangements.

It is just this identification of the son of man with our condition that became the authentic seal of his revelation of God. It was not an authority apart from his ministry which he bore; but it was the authority of the very incarnation of the spirit of ministry, that is, of a caring and bearing love, which became the foundation of the New Testament faith. Therefore, we who minister in his name cannot participate in the decisive word of truth which he brings on any other terms than to participate in his ministry. And that means to bear with the dark places of human experience, to face the unresolved problems, depending upon what God can and does do to make himself known in our life as we know it.

We can illustrate what this means in the work of those of us who go out as church musicians to enrich and strengthen the worship of Christian congregations. There are few things more needed than a strong, authoritative renewal of our Christian liturgies and our church music so that they will express the Christian story with joy and strength, and so that our worship is something other than a miscellaneous collection of things done from habit and from momentary inspiration. We have behind us the weight of 19 centuries of Christian liturgy and hymnology. We know there is an expression of Christian faith which gives voice to courage and joy and is not an orgy of soothing sentimentality. We have the centuries of theological authority behind our discrimination of hymn texts and we have our own trained sense, our musical and liturgical taste. We may be tempted to feel that such authority will be irresistible when it comes to setting Christian worship right. But we know that it is not irresistible. We can have all this authority on our side; but if we have not love and the spirit of ministry, it will not get us very far. Love here means the willingness to bear with those who are in all stages of Christian experience. It means the willingness even to bear with those who prefer old familiar hymn 97, no matter what. It means the willingness to lead and teach and point the way to the things that are excellent, and to believe that in time they will be heard and accepted.

III

Let us look at this view of authority in some areas of our ministries today. In the realm of Christian ethics there is a great wistfulness for an authority which will decide between right and wrong. Individuals and societies grow sick where there is nothing sure about moral practices.

The other day the Supreme Court refused to review the case of a Pennsylvania farmer who had been fined $94.00 for exceeding his 1954 wheat quota. The first amendment to the Constitution declares that no law shall prohibit the free exercise of religion, and it was his religious conviction that he should use his labor to realize the maximum productivity of his land. He thought he had the Constitution and his religious faith on his side; but the federal courts were on the other. Since the Supreme Court refused to review the case, they did not hand down a decision but it could have been a five to four decision. That symbolizes our situation as we search for justice. We make our way from decision to decision.

What, then, is the responsibility of the Christian minister? It is indeed to preach the absolute requirement of God's righteousness. It is to witness to the justice which is the foundation of a decent human society. But the moral authority which the gospel declares does not relieve us of the work of standing where the people stand who have to make decisions in our society and of taking upon ourselves the kinds of problems which form the stuff of human social existence.

A layman said to his minister a short time ago, "I appreciate your sermons, and I understand the validity of the requirements of the gospel; but my problem now is to live a Christian life and be an automobile salesman at the present time; especially a used car salesman."

We are saying that the moral authority in the gospel does not exempt us from recognizing the dilemmas of salesmen, or state department executives, or labor union rank and file members. They are our problems too. We have no right to make general moral pronouncements without going through the discipline of walking down the streets where men walk, and sitting with them as they make the kinds of choices which our world offers. If we minister in this spirit, we may have fewer general directives to give; but we may make a great gain in the realistic authority with which we speak the Christian word of love of neighbor.

There are issues where a courageous and costing stand for what we believe to be right must be taken. There are deep evils and injustices in every block, in every city, and in the relations of peoples and nations. But the kind of authority which the gospel gives us is that of a way, and a direction—a recognition of our own involvement in evil, and a call to costly decision as God gives us light.

IV

This principle that authority in the Christian faith requires the ministry of a patient acceptance of human problems holds in the sphere of Chirstian truth itself. There is a deep craving for authoritative religion in our day, and some are willing to be told what to believe. As John Milton observed long ago, "There is not any burden that some would gladlier post off to another, than the charge and care of their religion." Here again, we cannot have the kind of truth which Christ brings in its personal depth and mystery unless we are willing to ask the questions which every man asks, and the new questions which our generation asks about the meaning of our existence.

We are re-emphasizing today the authority of the Scripture at the base of our Protestant faith. The Bible, read with the witness of the Holy Spirit's presence, is not just another book full of noble sentiments and inspiring ideas. The words of Jesus, "Whoever would be first among you must be slave of all," is not just a wise saying from an ancient teacher. It is either the law of life which sooner or later confronts every man, or it is of no great importance. And when Paul writes, "You, who once were estranged and hostile in mind, doing evil deeds, he now has reconciled in his body of flesh by his death, in order to present you holy and blameless and unreproachable before him, provided that you continue in the faith," he is not merely describing a private experience or indulging in a noble speculation. Either he is speaking of a personal act of God which has created a new life and a new people in history, or it is of no great matter. The authority of the Scripture lies in its witness to what is real for us and for every man.

Yet we cannot have this authoritative word unless we are willing to engage in a continual search for its meaning in the midst of many perplexities. Surely the history of the Scripture proves that. The church has had to meet new scientific knowledge, new psychological knowledge, new historical research, and to ask again and again, What is the center of the biblical truth which stands above through all the changes of interpretations and understanding? The Bible does not automatically interpret itself.

In one of his brilliant essays David Roberts told of his discussion before the war with a young Nazi who saw no conflict between his Nazi beliefs and the Bible, and Dr. Roberts remarks: "What a man allows the Bible to say to him is profoundly influenced by the situation in which he finds himself."

We will not all agree as to how we approach the problem of biblical interpretation so as to expose our bias and error, but I do believe there is agreement among us that the Bible does not offer a detour around the problems of modern thought. The book is about the person of Jesus Christ, in whom all truth coheres. Therefore we are under obligation as his ministers to undergo the hard intellectual labor of seeking that coherence, and fearing no fact or truth, no matter where we find it.

The way in which we have been putting this matter may leave some of us unconvinced; for we seem to be saying that while ultimate authority lies with God, our sharing in his authoritative truth depends upon something we do, upon the faithfulness of our ministry, the adequacy of our intelligence. Surely there is something wrong with our witness if it means a pointing to ourselves, for we are generally poor examples of the truth and life we proclaim. Yet, if we make the authority of the ministry something external, something in no way related to our living and our personal faith, we remove it from all that counts in real human life.

There is an answer to this dilemma. It consists in reminding ourselves that the authority to which we point is not in our possessions, but one upon which we ourselves depend. When we preach the truth and power of the gospel, we do not say, "Look at us." We say we have experienced our own emptiness and we know him who fills our emptiness.

We are "in-between men," we Christians. We stand in between a grace which lays hold upon us, and our faltering human response. We stand in between the beginning of our Christian life and the end which comes only through working out our salvation with fear and trembling. We stand in between the clashing authorities of men and churches and governments, and that final and decisive word of God which has enabled men to defy all earthly authority in his name. There will always be a validity in those conceptions of the ministry which put the emphasis on the authority of the office, precisely because the minister points to the grace of God which is above our feeble embodiment of it.

There is then a discipline which is appropriate to those who minister in the name of Chirst. It is the discipline, not of self-congratulations, but of daily repentance. We stand as ministers under exactly the same need of grace as every other man. Whatever authority may attach to our preaching the gospel will depend upon our being clear about that.

It is the discipline of a constant act of self-identification with those who are hurt, sick, lost, or in any adversity. They are not poor people who need our help; they are Christ himself asking our love. He said, "As you did it to one of the least of these my brethren, you did it to me." Unless daily, with his help, we carry in our hearts the needs of all sorts and conditions of men, we cannot speak with authority of him who is the servant of all.

Christian ministry means a continual offering of gratitude and celebration. Nietzsche said, looking around at the Christianity he knew, "Christ's followers should look more redeemed." He was right. It is salvation that we preach. It is by the authority of God's victory over sin and death that we live. One of the Christian martyrs executed in the last days of the Hitler regime wrote to his family: "I thank you for having given me life. I never knew that dying is so easy. I die without any feeling of hatred." There is a quiet and final authority in such a witness which stands amid the wrecks of time.

May God, the Father of our Lord Jesus, go with us in our several ways, and keep us bound to one another in the fellowship of his church, and in this fellowship of teaching and learning, of joy and of faith, which has been ours in these days.

Biographical Sketch

REUEL HOWE

Reuel Howe is eminently qualified to preach to preachers. He is the Director of the Institute for Advanced Pastoral Studies at Bloomfield Hills, Michigan. After his graduation from Whitman College he studied at the Philadelphia Divinity School, where he received the degree S.T.D. Following his theological training he served in a Philadelphia parish and later as vicar of St. Stephens, Elsmere, New York.

He has spent many years in the training of the clergy. He was Professor of Pastoral Theology at Philadelphia Divinity School for seven years. Here he inaugurated a successful program of clinical pastoral training. At Virginia Theological Seminary he served for thirteen years as Professor of Pastoral Theology and developed a similar program. His present program is a postordination training center for pastors of all denominations.

He has pioneered in exploring the correlation of the findings of the psychological and sociological disciplines with theological insights. This has found expression in two very valuable books, *Man's Need and God's Action* and *The Creative Years*. He has also contributed to many journals in this field, served as a member of the Midcentury White House Conference on Children and Youth, and as guest lecturer at the Philadelphia Psychoanalytic Association, and as a member of the Board of Directors of the Washington School of Psychiatry and the Washington Seminar in Religion and Psychiatry.

Through the years he has been working with ministers in almost every capacity. He has met young ministers in the classroom, supervised them in clinical pastoral education programs, lectured to groups of pastors, written for them, preached to them, and counseled with them in vast numbers.

In a series on pastoral preaching, it seemed only logical that a sermon be included that was prepared with the needs of ministers in mind. Because of his rich and profound background in the training of the ministry, it was felt that Reuel Howe was one who would be especially qualified for such a task.

The
Miracle of Adequacy

Text: John 6:1-14

"WHO CAN BE EQUAL to the responsibility of being a minister in the Church of Christ?" is a question often asked by most men who have assumed that task. Some find a living answer to the question; others compromise the task and responsibility and manage to get by; and a few live in discouragement and despair, and either resign or endure the burden. The demands of the ministry are legion and crowd the clergy day and night. Anyone in the community, whether a member of his congregation or not, may appeal to him at any time about anything, often without warning and without regard for anything else he might be doing. Some demands are petty; others have a life-and-death urgency. Sometimes the importance of the demand is not obvious so that a minister may not know or be able to discover the seriousness of the situation. In short, the tasks seem very great, and the resources very small and inadequate.

The story of our Lord's feeding of the five thousand represents an overwhelming demand, pathetic resources, two experiences of inadequacy, and a miracle resulting from faith's application of the inadequate resources to a great problem. A study of that event may help us with our own problems.

Our Lord, in the midst of his teaching and healing, went to the other side of the Sea of Galilee. While he was there, he lifted up his eyes and saw that a great crowd of five thousand people had followed him because of his works of healing. With characteristic compassion he recognized their need, their fatigue, and their hunger; but being also a teacher, he recognized that the occasion offered an opportunity to give his disciples an examination. Turning to Philip and presumably to the rest of them, he asked: " 'How are we to buy bread, so that these people may eat?' " Or we might paraphrase his question as follows: "Here is a problem; I have been training you, now what would you do? Where can we find food that these may eat?" We know from the text that he was giving his disciples an examination because the writer of the Gospel further explains: "This he said to test him for he himself knew what he would do."

And so Philip, with the others, turned to study the problem. What could they do; what should they say? After sizing up the situation Philip responded: " 'Two hundred denarii would not buy enough bread for each of them to get a little.' " His reply indicated that he was overwhelmed by the task. He was intimidated by the vast crowd of people, by their hunger and fatigue, by their irritability and their restless expectations. The more he looked at them the more frightened he became and he could think only in terms of what he did not have. Philip did not do well in that particular examination, and his response has been repeated by disciples in all generations since. The Philip attitude is defeatism and tends to overestimate the difficulties of our problems. We see them as being larger and more complex than they are and as being too difficult to meet.

A certain Negro woman in a Southern town is known to have said about racial prejudice and injustice, "It's jes too big, a body cain't do nothin about it. People ain't going to change." And all of us may say the same thing about personal problems, about difficulties in church relations, about community and national problems. Many clergy seem to be bowed down by the problems of administration, by those that grow out of their relation with their people, and those created by relations with the community. And, like Philip, we can become so preoccupied with the problems of life that we are blind to any resources that might be available.

While Philip was responding, Andrew, Simon Peter's brother, was doing some "last-minute cramming," and getting ready to make his response to the test. He did a little better. Whereas Philip saw only problems, Andrew saw some resources. He said, " 'There is a lad here who has five barley loaves and two fish.' " But then he spoiled his response by adding, " 'but what are they among so many?' " Whereas Philip was overwhelmed by the enormity of the task, Andrew was unimpressed by what he had to work with; he underestimated the potential of his resources. Modern disciples, too, make the Andrew response to the testings of life. The Negro woman who made the earlier comment about the size and complexity of the race problem also said, "There ain't nothin I can do about it, I'se only one person." Many times we have said the same thing. We look at ourselves and estimate what we can do, and become discouraged. We look at other people and fail to see their possibilities. When a situation seems to call for love, our love does not seem to be very good, very strong, or equal to the task. We are tempted to say, "It isn't enough." We may look at the church in relation to the world to which it is sent and underestimate it as a resource. It is too weak, too sinful, too unrelated. We profess belief in the sacraments, but the power of grace seems ineffectual when compared with atomic power . . . and our faith fails us.

It would be bad enough to be either a Philip or an Andrew, but the truth is we often combine both responses in our living. We both overestimate our difficulties and underestimate our resources. A recent issue of a popular magazine carried an article entitled, "Why I Quit the

Ministry" in which an anonymous young minister's Philip and Andrew responses were described. The inevitable effect of two such attitudes is defeat in which a sense of inadequacy overwhelms the possibilities of life.

So far in our story no miracles have occurred, but now our Lord, who is Savior as well as teacher, faces the test he gave his disciples and passes it for them.

Jesus said, "'Make the people sit down.'" He did not overestimate the difficulties of the situation; he did not pretend that they were not there, nor did he evade them in any way. There were five thousand hungry, tired, and irritable people that needed help, and he accepted the situation by saying, "Make the people sit down." It is one thing to have five thousand hungry people on foot; it is another thing to have five thousand hungry people seated on the grass at your invitation and waiting for something to happen. The invitation to sit down reveals his acceptance of the problem. We cannot begin to meet any of the challenges and problems of life until we first accept them as belonging to us. The acceptance of the situation is the first step in the working of miracles. Our own experience reveals this truth to us. The longer we put off facing responsibilities, the bigger they seem to get. When we finally decide that the time has come to act and do something about a difficult situation, the problem often seems more possible to accomplish. It does not seem to be as big as it was while we were pushing it off. We begin to feel better, too, because we are no longer evading something that we know is ours.

The second step in the miracle is demonstrated by our Lord's next action. "Jesus then took the loaves and . . . fish." His acceptance of them, even though they were very few and obviously inadequate for the task, was typical of our Lord. Not only did he accept and use the pathetically few loaves and fish, but he also called, accepted and depended upon most unpromising people, including ourselves. His acceptance of us and other resources for the accomplishment of his miracles may encourage us to be more accepting of ourselves and others. The Negro woman who thought the race problem was too big to handle and who felt there was nothing that she could do about it because she was only one ignorant person, decided one day not to move from the white section of a bus in the Southern town where she lived. She was put off, arrested, and precipitated a response from hundreds of people who brought the issue squarely before the whole community, and convicted and quickened consciences that made men decide where they stood in relation to a matter of justice. Her little life and her little action ignited the entire community. By accepting what we are and have, and by using it with faith we begin to grow. A new sense of being and power for living begins to emerge, and our spirit begins to respond with courage to the threats to our life. Miracles begin to happen. Hope overcomes despair, love redeems hate, and life overcomes death even when the resources for the working of the miracle seem pitifully inadequate.

A third step in the working of miracles is demonstrated by our Lord when he gave thanks for what he had. It would not be untrue to his spirit and way of acting to think that he gave thanks for the five thousand hungry people as well as for the loaves and fish, because of the opportunity it gave him to glorify his Father.

Our own experience reveals that the whole picture of our life can be transformed when we not only accept our problems and resources but also give thanks for them. We all remember times when some crisis overtook us that seemed to blight the promise of our lives. And yet, when we met the crisis with courage, we could look back on it and see that a great blessing had come out of it, that a relationship was deepened only because we faced the crisis and dared to give ourselves and use our other resources. If we can look back and see that this kind of miracle really happened, our faith in miracles will increase. Miracle-working Christian living is the capacity to face life with the expectation that if we will accept and give thanks for the problems and resources of life, we will see a miracle of adequacy replace the defeatism of inadequacy.

A fourth and final step in our Lord's working of the miracle was that he acted in faith: he distributed the loaves and fish to those who were hungry. Having accepted and given thanks for his resources, he used them. After all the preparation, after the acceptance and thanksgiving, there comes the moment finally when we must act. This is when we are tempted to draw back. Prior to this point we can always believe that our purposes will be accomplished, that our resources will be adequate, and that the response will be cooperative. But when we come to the moment of action, we have to commit ourselves, distribute the bread, take the risk of applying our resources to our problem in the faith that the miracle will occur. We are afraid of the risk of action, afraid that what we do will not be good enough, that the miracle will not "come off." But here our Lord reassures us. In effect he says, "Accept what you have, give thanks for it, and now in faith use it, give it, and depend on me."

The rest of his act of faith is expressed in these words from the story: "And when they had eaten their fill, he told his disciples, 'Gather up the fragments left over, that nothing may be lost.' So they gathered them up and filled twelve baskets with fragments from the five barley loaves, left by those who had eaten." Thus we see that the action was not barely adequate but was overflowingly adequate. We, too, have experienced this and known times when that which was done was far in excess of anything we had reason to expect.

We are not called upon to accomplish the miracles out of our own power. Now, as then, our Lord wrought them.

Our ministry is not one in which we have to do God's work for him. Ours is a ministry of participating in what he is doing. In this incident he tells us that we participate in what he is doing by accepting our problems, by accepting our resources, by giving thanks for them, and finally by giving ourselves in responsible action in the faith that through us more will be accomplished than we had thought possible. The day of miracles is still with us.

PART IV

So Great
a Cloud of Witnesses

Sermons from the masters

> *Therefore since we are surrounded by so great
> a cloud of witnesses, let us also lay aside every
> weight, and sin which clings so closely, and
> let us run with perseverance the race that is
> set before us.*
>
> —Hebrews 12:1

When the author of the Book of Hebrews wanted to restore the faith and deepen the courage of his readers, who were facing a most difficult situation, he did so by referring to the heroes of the past. He mentioned Abel and Enoch and Noah and Abraham and Moses and David and Samuel, and many more. If they could recall the courage and faith of their forefathers, he said, it would give them courage and strength to run the race that was before them.

The pastor, too, at times needs to remember the great heritage of which he is a part. It gives him a sense of perspective and purpose as he faces the task that is before him. It is a great thing to stand in the line of Chrysostom and Luther and Wesley and Spurgeon and Chalmers and Robertson and Brooks and Gordon and others too numerous to mention. The pastor, too, is "Surrounded by a great cloud of witnesses."

Much practical help that can be secured from a knowledge of what they did and an understanding of their motives and methods. When Dr. Fosdick was going through the personal struggle we mentioned earlier, when he was floundering around, trying to find some approach to preaching that was vital and real, he discovered that much could be learned by a study of the masters. He studied their sermons carefully, meticulously, thoroughly. As a result, he said, "While we modern preachers talk about psychology much more than our predecessors, we commonly use it a good deal less."[1]

In this final section we include two sermons by men of a former generation as illustrations of this capacity of which Dr. Fosdick speaks. The possibilities of choice at this point were almost endless, but a choice had to be made somewhere. Of the hundreds that might have been chosen, we selected a sermon preached by Horace Bushnell almost ninety years ago, and one preached by Washington Gladden fifty-nine years ago. Their names are familiar but few people read their sermons today. Yet, when we do read these sermons, we have the feeling that with minor revisions these ideas are as relevant now as they were then.

---

[1]Fosdick, *The Living of These Days*, p. 100.

HORACE BUSHNELL

Horace Bushnell's sermon, "Every Man's Life a Plan of God," has been declared by one church historian to be one of the three greatest sermons of modern times. This is quite a statement when one considers the fact that more than 300,000 sermons are preached in America every Sunday of the year. Any sermon that is included in the top three has endured quite a test.

Bushnell is recognized as a great preacher. This was true almost from the beginning. Many in the field of homiletics say that he has influenced preaching in America as much as any one man. Known as a "preachers' preacher," he had a profound influence on the thought and methods of such pulpit giants as Phillips Brooks, Washington Gladden, and George Gordon. Bushnell has been compared to Jonathan Edwards who dominated the thought of an earlier generation; in fact, many would say that Bushnell marked the beginning of a new era in preaching.

He is best known for his classical book, *Christian Nurture,* which, although controversial in its day, has been extremely influential in the whole field of religious education and the psychology of religion. Perhaps Bushnell thought of himself, however, more as a preacher and theologian, although he was never a professional theologian, certainly not a systematic one and, Sweet would say, not even a learned one. Nonetheless, his influence on the theological thought of his generation was widespread and it is in understanding his approach to theology that we gain an insight into his approach to preaching, which, in turn, reveals the relationship of both to human need.

Gaius Glenn Atkins says of his thinking, "The age he inherited approached life through doctrine. He approached doctrine through life."

Amos S. Chesebrough described Bushnell's theological thought in these words,

Christian doctrine was to him no longer a conclusion from a process of reasoning, but it was formulated Christian experience. It must be, not a speculation, not a piece of well-reasoned framework which nicely fits into a theological system, but something to live by—something firstly, secondly, always, vitally practical for the uses of the soul.[1]

This is also a description of his purposes in preaching. Many of Dr. Bushnell's sermons could be selected that show how he met these practical needs of the soul and reveal his psychological insights that were far in advance of his day. The sermon we include here is the one mentioned above. It was apparently one which Bushnell himself held in high regard, for when he published a volume of sermons that were representative of 25 years of his preaching, *Preaching for the New Life,* he selected this sermon to appear first.

[1]From *Bushnell Centenary,* p. 47.

Every Man's
Life a Plan of God

"I girded thee, though thou hast not known me."
—Isaiah 45:5[1]

So BEAUTIFUL is the character and history of Cyrus, the person here addressed, that many have doubted whether the sketch given by Xenophon was not intended as an idealizing or merely romantic picture. And yet there have been examples of as great beauty unfolded here and there in all the darkest recesses of the heathen world, and it accords entirely with the hypothesis of historic verity in the account given us of this remarkable man that he is designated and named by our prophet, even before he is born, as a chosen foster-son of God. "I have surnamed thee," he declares, "I girded thee, though thou hast not known me." And what should he be but a model of all princely beauty, of bravery, of justice, of impartial honor to the lowly, of greatness and true magnanimity in every form, when God has girded him, unseen, to be the minister of his own great and sovereign purposes to the nations of his time.

Something of the same kind will also be detected in the history and personal consciousness of almost every great and remarkable character. Christ himself testifies to the girding of the Almighty when he says: "To this end was I born, and for this cause came I into the world." Abraham was girded for a particular work and mission in what is otherwise denominated his call. Joseph in Egypt distinguishes the girding of God's hand when he

---

[1]Scripture references in this sermon are from the King James version.

comforts his guilty brothers in the assurance: "So it was not you that sent me hither, but God." Moses and Samuel were called by name, and set to their great lifework in the same manner. What is Paul endeavoring in all the stress and pressure of his mighty apostleship but to perform the work for which God's Spirit girded him at his call, and to apprehend that for which he was apprehended of Christ Jesus? And yet these great master-spirits of the world are not so much distinguished by the acts they do as by the sense itself of some mysterious girding of the Almighty upon them whose behests they are set on to fulfill. All men may have this, for the humblest and commonest have a place and a work assigned them in the same manner, and are privileged to be always ennobled in the same lofty consciousness. God is girding every man for a place and a calling in which he may be as consciously exalted as if he held the rule of a kingdom even though the task be internally humble. The truth I propose then for your consideration is this: *God has a definite life plan for every human person, girding him, visibly or invisibly, for some exact thing which it will be the true significance and glory of his life to have accomplished.*

Many persons, I am well aware, never even think of any such thing. They suppose that for most men life is a necessarily stale and common affair. What it means for them they do not know, and they scarcely conceive that it means anything. They even complain, venting heavy sighs, that, while some few are set forward by God to do great works and fill important places, they are not allowed to believe that there is any particular object in their existence. It is remarkable, considering how generally this kind of impression prevails, that the holy Scriptures never give way to it, but seem as it were in all possible ways to be holding up the dignity of common life and giving a meaning to its appointments which the natural dullness and lowness of mere human opinion cannot apprehend.

The Scriptures not only show us explicitly, as we have seen, that God has a definite purpose in the lives of men already great, but they show us, in the conditions of obscurity and depression, preparations of counsel going on by which the commonest offices are to become the necessary first chapter of a great and powerful history. David among the sheep; Elisha following after the plough; Nehemiah bearing the cup; Hannah, who can say nothing less common than that she is the wife of Elkanah and a woman of a sorrowful spirit—who that looks on these humble people at their post of service and discovers at last how dear a purpose God was cherishing in them, can be justified in thinking that God has not a particular plan for him because he is not signalized by any kind of distinction?

Besides, what do the Scriptures show us that God has a particular care for every man, a personal interest in him and a sympathy with him and his trials, watching for the uses of his one talent as attentively and kindly, and approving him as heartily in the right employment of it as if he had given him ten? What is the giving out of the talents itself but an exhibition of the fact that God has a definite purpose, charge, and work, be it this or that, for every man?

They also make it the privilege of every man to live in the secret guidance of God, which is plainly nugatory unless there is some chosen work or sphere into which he may be guided; for how shall God guide him, having nothing appointed or marked out for him to be guided into, no field opened for him, no course set down which is to be his wisdom?

God also professes in his word to have purposes prearranged for all events, to govern by a plan which is from eternity even, and which in some proper sense

comprehends everything. What is this but another way
of conceiving that God has a definite place and plan adjusted for every human being? Without such a plan he
could not govern the world intelligently or make a proper
universe of the created system, for it becomes a universe
only in the grand unity of reason which includes it.
Otherwise it were only a jumble of fortuities without
counsel, end, or law.

Turning now from the Scriptures to the works of God,
how constantly are we met here by the fact, everywhere
visible, that ends and uses are the regulative reasons of
all existing things. This we discover often, when we are
least able to understand the speculative mystery of objects; for it is precisely the uses of things that are most
palpable. These uses are to God, no doubt, as to us, the
significance of his works. They compose, taken together,
a grand reciprocal system in which part answers actively
to part, constructing thus an all-comprehensive and
glorious whole. The system is, in fact, so perfect that the
loss or displacement of any member would fatally de-
range the general order. If there were any smallest star
in heaven that had no place to fill, that oversight would
beget a disturbance which no Leverrier could compute
because it would be a real and eternal, and not merely
a casual or apparent disorder. One grain, more or less, of
sand would disturb or even fatally disorder the whole
scheme of the heavenly motions. So nicely balanced and
so carefully hung are the worlds that even the grains of
their dust are counted, and their places adjusted to a
correspondent nicety. There is nothing included in the
gross or total sum that could be dispensed with. The same
is true in regard to forces that are apparently irregular.
Every particle of air is moved by laws of as great pre-
cision as the laws of the heavenly bodies, or indeed by
the same laws; keeping its appointed place and serving
its appointed use. Every odor exhales in the nicest con-

formity with its appointed place and law. Even the view-
less and mysterious heat stealing through the dark center
and impenetrable depths of the worlds obeys its uses
with unfaltering exactness, dissolving never so much as
an atom that was not to be dissolved. What now shall
we say of men appearing, as it were, in the center of this
great circle of uses? They are all adjusted for him; has
he, then, no ends appointed for himself? Noblest of all
creatures and closest to God as he certainly is, are we to
say that his Creator has no definite thoughts concerning
him, no place prepared for him to fulfill, no use for him
to serve, which is the reason of his existence?

There is, then, I conclude, a definite and proper end
or issue for every man's existence; an end which, to the
heart of God, is the good intended for him or for which
he was intended; that which he is privileged to become,
called to become, ought to become; that which God will
assist him to become and which he cannot miss save by
his own fault. Every human soul has a complete and perfect plan cherished for him in the heart of God—a divine
biography marked out which it enters into life to live.
This life, rightly unfolded, will be a complete and beautiful whole, an experience led on by God and unfolded
by his secret nurture, as the trees and the flowers by the
secret nurture of the world; a drama cast in the mold of
a perfect art, with no part wanting; a divine study for
the man himself and for others; a study that shall forever
unfold in wondrous beauty the love and faithfulness of
God; great in its conception, great in the divine skill by
which it is shaped, above all great in the momentous and
glorious issues it prepares. What a thought is this for
every human soul to cherish! What dignity does it add
to life! What support does it bring to the trials of life!
What instigations does it add to send us onward in
everything that constitutes our excellence! We live in the
divine thought. We fill a place in the great everlasting

plan of God's intelligence. We never sink below his care, never drop out of his counsel.

There is, I must add, a single but very important and even fearful qualification. Things all serve their uses and never break out of their places. They have no power to do it. Not so with us. We are able, as free beings, to refuse the place and duties God appoints; and, if we do, then we sink into something lower than and unworthy of us. That highest and best condition for which God designed us is no more possible. We have fallen out of it and we cannot wholly recover it. And yet, as that was the best thing possible for us in the reach of God's original counsel, so there is a place designed for us now, which is the next best possible. God calls us now to the best thing left, and will do so till all good possibility is narrowed down and spent. And then, when he cannot use us any more for our own good, he will use us for the good of others—an example of the misery and horrible desperation to which any soul must come when all the good ends and all the holy callings of God's friendly and fatherly purpose are exhausted. Or it may be now that, remitting all other plans and purposes in our behalf, he will henceforth use us, wholly against our will, to be the demonstration of his justice and avenging power before the eyes of mankind; saying over us, as he said over Pharaoh in the day of his judgments: "Even for this same purpose have I raised thee up, that I might show my power in thee and that my name might be declared throughout all the earth." Doubtless he had other and more genial plans to serve in this bad man, if only he could have accepted such; but knowing his certain rejection of these, God turned his mighty counsel in him wholly on the use to be made of him as a reprobate. How many Pharaohs in common life refuse every other use God will make of them, choosing only to figure in their small way as reprobates, and descending in that manner to a fate that painfully mimics his!

God has then, I conclude, a definite life plan set for every man—one that, being accepted and followed, will conduct him to the best and noblest end possible. No qualification of this doctrine is needed save the fearful one just named—that we, by our perversity, often refuse to take the place and do the work he gives us.

It follows in the same way that, as God in fixing on our end or use will choose the best end or use possible, so he will appoint for us the best manner possible of attaining it; for, as it is a part of God's perfection to choose the best things and not things partially good, so it will be in all the methods he prescribes for their attainment. And so, as we pass on stage by stage in our courses of experience, it is made clear to us that whatever we have laid upon us to do or to suffer, whatever to want, whatever to surrender or to conquer, is exactly best for us. Our life is a school exactly adapted to our lesson, and that to the best, last end of our existence.

No room for a discouraged or depressed feeling therefore is left us. Enough that we exist for a purpose high enough to give meaning to life and to support a genuine inspiration. If our sphere is outwardly humble, if it even appears to be quite insignificant, God understands it better than we do, and it is a part of his wisdom to bring out great sentiments in humble conditions, great principles in works that are outwardly trivial, great characters under great adversities and heavy loads of incumbrance. The tallest saints of God will often be those who walk in the deepest obscurity and are even despised or quite overlooked by man. Let it be enough that God is in our history, that the plan of our biography is his, and the issue he has set for it the highest and the best. Let us be filled with cheerfulness and exalted feeling, however deep in obscurity our lot may be, that God is leading us on, girding us for a work, preparing us to a good that is worthy of his divine magnificence. If God is really preparing us all to become that which is the very highest and best thing possible, there ought never to be a discouraged or uncheerful being in the world.

Nor is it any detraction from such a kind of life that the helm of its guidance is, by the supposition, to be in God and not in our own will and wisdom. This, in fact, is its dignity: it is a kind of divine order, a creation molded by the loving thoughts of God; in that view to the man himself a continual discovery, as it is unfolded, both of himself and God. A discovery of some kind it must be to all; for however resolutely or defiantly we undertake to accomplish our own objects and cut our own way through to a definite self-appointed future, it will never be true for one moment that we are certain of this future, and it will almost always be true that we are met by changes and conditions unexpected. This, in fact, is one of the common mitigations even of a selfish and self-directed life—that its events come up out of the unknown and overtake the subject as discoveries he could neither shun nor anticipate. Evil itself is far less evil even to the worldly man since it comes by surprises. Were the scenes of necessary bitterness, wrong, trial, disappointment, self-accusation that every such man has to pass through in his life distinctly set before him at the beginning, how forbidding generally, and how dismal the prospect! We frequently say therefore, "I could not have endured these distasteful, painful years, these emptinesses, these trials and torments that have rent me one after another, if I had definitely known beforehand what kind of lot was before me." And yet it is poor comfort to such pains and disasters that they overtook the sufferer as surprises and sorrows not set down beforehand in the self-appointed program of life. How different, how inspiring and magnificent, instead, to live by holy consent a life all discovery; to see it unfolding moment by moment a plan of God, our own life plan conceived in his paternal love; each event, incident, experience, whether bright or dark, having its mission from him and revealing, either now or in its future issues, the magnificence of his favoring counsel; to be sure in the dark day of a light that will follow; that loss will terminate in gain; that trial will issue in rest; doubt in satisfaction, suffering in patience, patience in purity; and all in a consummation of greatness and dignity that even God will look on with a smile. How magnificent, how strong in its repose, how full of rest is such a life! Call it human, decry it, let it down by whatever diminutives can be invented, still it is great; a charge which ought to inspire even a dull-minded man with energy and holy enthusiasm.

The inquiry will be made: Supposing all this to be true in the manner stated, how can we ever get hold of this life plan God has made for us, or find our way into it? Here to many if not to all will be the main stress of doubt and practical suspense.

Let us observe then, some negatives that are important and must be avoided.

We will never come into God's plan if we study singularity, for if God has a design or plan for every man's life, then it is exactly appropriate to his nature; and as every man's nature is singular and peculiar to himself—as peculiar as his face or look—then it follows that God will lead him into a singular, original, and peculiar life without any study of singularity on his part. Let us seek to be just what God would have us, and what the talents, the duties, and the circumstances of our lives will require us to be, and then we will be just peculiar enough. We will have a life of our own, a life that is naturally and therefore healthily peculiar; a simple, unaffected, unambitious life whose plan is not in ourselves, but in God.

As little will we seek to copy the life of another. No man is ever called to be another. God has as many plans for men as he has men, and therefore he never requires them to measure their life exactly by any other life. We are not to require it of ourselves to have the precise feelings or exercises, or do the works, or pass through the trials of other men, for God will handle us according to what we are, and not according to what other men are. We will find it impossible to be exercised by any given fashion, or to be any given character such as we know or have read of, even as it is impossible to make ourselves another nature. God's plan must hold and we must seek no other. To strain after something new and peculiar is fantastic and weak, and is also as nearly wicked as that kind of weakness can be. To be a copyist working at the reproduction of a human model is to have no faith in our significance, to judge that God means nothing in our particular lives, but only in the life of some other man. Submitting ourselves in this manner to the fixed opinion that our lives mean nothing, and that nothing is left for us but to borrow or beg a life plan from some other man, we as copyist become nothing but an affectation or a dull imposture.

In this view also we are never to complain of our birth, our training, our employments, our hardships; never to fancy that we could be something if on'y we had a different lot and sphere assigned us. God understands his own plan, and he knows what we want a great deal better than we do. The very things that we deprecate most as fatal limitations or obstructions are probably what we want most. What we call hindrances, obstacles, discouragements, are probably God's opportunities; it is nothing new that the patient should dislike his medicines, or any certain proof that they are poisons. No! A truce to all such impatience! Let us choke that devilish envy which gnaws at our hearts because we are not in the same lot with others; let us bring down our soul, or rather bring it up, to receive God's will and do his work in our lot, in our sphere, under our cloud of obscurity, against our temptations; and then we will find that our condition is never opposed to our good, but really consistent with it. Thus it was that an apostle required his converts to abide each one in that calling wherein he was called; to fill his place till by filling it he opened a way to some other; the bondman to fill his house of bondage with love and duty, the laborer to labor, the woman to be a woman, the men to show themselves men—all to acknowlege God's hand in their lot, and seek to cooperate with that good design which he most assuredly cherishes for them.

Another point to be carefully guarded is that, while we surrender and renounce all thought of making up a plan or choosing out a plan for ourselves as one that we set by our own will, we also give up the hope or expectation that God will set us in any scheme of life where the whole course of it will be known or set down beforehand. If we go to him to be guided, he will guide us, but he will not comfort our distrust, or half trust of him by showing us the chart of all his purposes concerning us. He will only show us into a way where, if we go cheerfully and trustfully forward, he will show us on still farther. No contract will be made with us, save that he engages, if we trust him, to lead us into the best things all the way through. And if they are better than we can either ask or think beforehand, they will be none the worse for that.

We must not stop in negatives. How then, or by what more positive directions can we who really desire to do it come into the plan God lays for us, so as to live it and rationally believe that we do? We are on the point of choosing, it may be, this or that calling, wanting to know where duty lies and what the course God himself would have us take.

Beginning at a point most remote and where the generality of truth is widest, let us consider (1) the character of God, and we will draw a large deduction from that; for all that God designs for us will be in harmony with his character. He is a being infinitely good, just, true. Therefore we are to know that he cannot really seek anything contrary to this in us. We may make ourselves contrary in every attribute of character to God; but he never made us become anything different from or unworthy of himself. A good being could not make another to be a bad being, as the proper issue and desired end of his existence; least of all could a being infinitely good. A great many employments or callings are by these first principles forever cut off. No thought is permitted us, even for a moment, of any work or calling that does not represent the industry, justice, truth, beneficence, mercy of God.

(2) Let us consider our relation to him as a creature. All created wills have their natural center and rest in God's will. In him they all come into a play of harmony, and the proper harmony of being is possible only in this way. Thus we know that we are called to have a will perfectly harmonized with God's and rested in his, and that gives us a large insight into what we are to be or what is the real end of our being. In fact nine tenths of our particular duties may be settled at once by a simple reference in this manner to what God wills.

(3) We have a conscience which is given to be an interpreter of his will and thus of our duty, and, in both, of what we are to become.

(4) God's law and his written word are guides to present duty which, if faithfully accepted, will help set us in accordance with the mind of God and the plan he has laid for us. "I am a stranger in the earth," said one, "hide not thy commandments from me"; knowing that God's commandments would give him a clue to the true meaning and business of his life.

(5) Be an observer of Providence, for God is showing us ever, by the way in which he leads us, whither he means to lead. Let us study our trials, our talents, the world's wants, and stand ready to serve God now in whatever he brings to our hands.

Again (6) let us consult our friends, and especially those who are most in the teaching of God. They know our talents and personal qualifications better in some respects than we do ourselves. Let us ask their judgment of us and of the spheres and works to which we are best adapted.

Once more (7) let us go to God himself and ask for the calling of God; for as certainly as he has a plan or calling for us, he will somehow guide us into it. And this is the proper office and work of his Spirit. By this private teaching he can and will show us into the very plan that is set for us. This is the significance of what is prescribed as our duty, namely, living and walking in the Spirit; for the Spirit of God is a kind of universal presence or inspiration in the world's bosom, an unfailing inner light, which if we accept and live in, we are guided into a consenting choice so that what God wills for us we also will for ourselves, settling into it as the needle to the pole. By this hidden union with God or intercourse with him, we get a wisdom or insight deeper than we know and love. We go into the very plan of God for us and are led along in it by him, consenting, cooperating, answering to him, we know not how, and working out with nicest exactness that good end for which his unseen counsel girded us and sent us into the world. In this manner, not neglecting the other methods just named, but gathering in all their separate lights to be interpreted in the higher light of the Spirit, we can never be greatly at a loss to find our way into God's counsel and plan. The duties of the present moment we shall meet as they rise, and these will open a gate into the next, and we shall thus pass on trustfully and securely, almost never in doubt as to what God calls us to do.

It is not to be supposed that my readers have followed me in such a subject as this without encountering questions from within that are piercing. It has put them on reflection; it has set them to the inquiry what they have been doing and becoming thus far in their course, and what they are hereafter to be. Ten, twenty, fifty, seventy years ago we came into this living world and began to breathe this mortal air. The guardian angel that came to take charge of us said: "To this end is he born, for this cause is he come into the world." Or if this be a Jewish fancy, God said the same himself. He had a definite plan for us, a good end settled and cherished for us in his heart. This it was that gave a meaning and a glory to our lives. Apart from this it was not, in his view, life for us to live; it was accident, frustration, death.

What now, O soul, hast thou done? What progress hast thou made? How much of the blessed life plan of thy Father hast thou executed? How far on the way art thou to the good, best end thy God has designed for thee?

Do I hear thy soul confessing with a suppressed sob within thee that, up to this time, thou hast never sought God's chosen plan at all? Hast thou, even to this hour and during so many years been following a way and a plan of thine own, regardless hitherto of all God's purposes in thee? If it be so, what hast thou gotten? How does thy plan work? Does it bring thee peace, content, dignity of aim and feeling, purity, rest; or does it plunge thee into mires of disturbance, scorch thee in flames of passion, worry thee with cares, burden thee with bitter reflections, cross thee, disappoint, sadden, sour thee? And what are thy prospects? What is the issue to come? After thou hast worked out this hard plan of thine own, will it come to a good end? Hast thou courage now to go on and work it through?

Perhaps we may be entertaining ourselves for the time with a notion of our prosperity, counting ourselves happy in past successes and counting on greater successes to come. Do we call it then success that we are getting on in a plan of our own? There cannot be a greater delusion. We set up a plan that is not God's and rejoice that it seems to prosper, not observing that we are just as much farther off from God's plan for us and from all true wisdom as we seem to prosper more. The day is coming when just this truth will be revealed to us as the bitterest pang of our defeat and shame.

No matter which it be, prosperity or acknowledged defeat, the case is much the same in one as in the other if we stand apart from God and his counsel. There is nothing good preparing for any man who will not live in God's plan. If he goes prospecting for himself and will not apprehend that for which he is apprehended, it cannot be to any good purpose.

And really I know not anything, my hearers, more sad and painful to think of, to a soul properly enlightened by reason and God's truth, than so many years of divine good squandered and lost; whole years, possibly many years, of that great and blessed biography which God designed for us, occupied by a frivolous and foolish invention of our own, substituted for the good counsel of God's infinite wisdom and love.

For the young man or woman, this is the day of hope. All his best opportunities are still before him. Now, too, he is laying his plans for the future. Why not lay them in God? Who has planned for all as wisely and faithfully as he? Let the young man's life begin with him. Let him believe that he is girded by his God for a holy and great calling. Let him go to God and consecrate his life to him, knowing assuredly that he will lead him into just that life which is his highest honor and blessing.

What shall I say to the older man who is farther on
in his courses and is still without God in the world? The
beginning of wisdom he has yet to learn. He has really
done nothing as yet that he was sent into the world to do.
All his best opportunities too are gone or going by. The
best end, the next best and the next are gone, and nothing
but the dregs of opportunity is left. And still Christ calls
even him. There is a place still left for him; not the best
and brightest, but a humble and good one. To this he
is called, for this he is apprehended of Christ Jesus still.
Let him repent of his dusty and dull and weary way, and
take the call that is offered.

All men living without God are adventurers out upon
God's world, in neglect of him, to choose their own
course. Hence the sorrowful, sad-looking host they make.
O that I could show them whence their bitterness, their
dryness, their unutterable sorrows come! O that I could
silence for one hour the noisy tumult of their works and
get them to look in upon that better, higher life of fruit-
fulness and blessing to which their God has appointed
them! Will they ever see it? Alas, I fear!

Friends of God, disciples of the Son of God, how inspiring and magnificent the promise or privilege that is offered here to us! It may seem impossible that we can ever
find our way into a path prepared for us by God and be
led along in it by his mighty counsel. To do this requires
a very close, well-kept life, a life in which the soul can
have confidence always toward God, a life which allows
the Spirit always to abide and reign, driven away by no
affront of selfishness. There must be a complete renuncia-
tion of self-will. God and religion must be practically first,
and the testimony that we please God must be the element of our peace. Such a disciple I have never known
who did not have it for his joy that God was leading him
on, shaping his life for him, bringing him along out of
one moment into the next, year by year. To such a disciple

there is nothing strained or difficult in saying that God's plan can be found, or that this is the true mode and privilege of life. Nothing to him is easier or more natural. He knows that God is ever present, feels that God determines all things for him, rejoices in the confidence that the everlasting counsel of his Friend is shaping every turn of his experience. He does not go hunting after this confidence; it comes to him, abides in him, fortifies his breast, and makes his existence itself an element of peace. And this is our privilege, if only we can live close enough to have the secret of the Lord with us.

How sacred, how strong in its repose, how majestic, how nearly divine is a life thus ordered! The simple thought of a life which is to be the unfolding in this manner of a divine plan, is too beautiful, too captivating, to suffer one indifferent or heedless moment. Living in this manner, every turn of our experience will be a discovery of God, every change a token of his fatherly counsel. Whatever obscurity, darkness, trial, suffering falls upon us; our defeats, losses, injuries; our outward state, employment, relations; what seems hard, unaccountable, severe or, as nature might say, vexatious,—all these we will see are parts or constitutive elements in God's beautiful and good plan for us, and as such are to be accepted with a smile. If we have an implicit trust in God, these very things will impart the highest zest to life. If we were in our own will, we could not bear them; and if we fall at any time into our own will, they will break us down. But the glory of our condition as a Christian is that we are in the mighty and good will of God. Bunyan called his hero Greatheart, for no heart can be weak that is in the confidence of God. Paul counted all things but loss for the excellency of the knowledge; endured with godlike patience unspeakable sufferings; cast everything behind him and followed on to apprehend that for which he was apprehended. He had a great and mighty will,

but no self-will; therefore he was strong, a true lion of
the faith. Away then with all feeble complaints, all mea-
ger and mean anxieties. Let us take our duty and be
strong in it, as God will make us strong. The harder it is,
the stronger in fact we will be. We must understand also
that the great question here is not what we will get, but
what we will become. The greatest wealth we can ever
get will be in ourselves. Let us take our burdens and
troubles and losses and wrongs, if come they must and
will, as our opportunities, knowing that God has girded
us for greater things than these. O to live out such a life
as God appoints, how great a thing it is!—to do the duties,
make the sacrifices, bear the adversities, finish the plan,
and then to say with Christ (who of us will be able?),
"It is finished!"

Biographical Sketch

WASHINGTON GLADDEN

Washington Gladden is best known as a social prophet, one of the pioneers in the social gospel movement, author of the hymn, "O Master Let Me Walk with Thee." He also was an outstanding pastor; in fact, he was selected to contribute the volume *The Christian Pastor* to the series of books so influential in theological training a generation ago, *The International Theological Series*.

In this volume he presents his concept of preaching and pastoral work. A few quotations reveal something of his spirit and the relationship between these two primary functions of the minister. Though this appeared in 1898, it sounds most contemporary; in fact, it can be applied without comment or interpretation:

The minister's throne is his pulpit. . . . A great many kinds of work are now expected of the minister, and some of them are of great importance; but the minister makes a great mistake who permits his pulpit work to take a secondary place. Christ said that the one supreme purpose of his mission to the world was that he might bear witness to the truth; and the same must always be the high calling of the servant of Christ. . . . Men are saved from being conformed to this world only when they are transformed by the renewing of their minds; and it is the minister's chief business to keep their minds well supplied with the truth by which this transformation is wrought.

He thought of preaching as a message not to a crowd but to persons:

Let us think of his [the pastor's] preaching as a message to the individual. It used to be said that the chief end of preaching is the salvation of souls. If these terms are rightly understood, no fault can be found with them. A soul is a man; and there can be no question that a great many men are in danger of being lost, and that all men are worth saving. . . . The minister is preaching then to save men—to save them from sin and sorrow and shame; to save them from losses that are irreparable; to save them for lives of honor and nobility, and for the service of humanity. The longer any earnest minister lives, the more deeply he will feel the need of such preaching as this—the more earnestly he will long for the power to speak the persuasive word which shall turn men from the ways of death to the ways of life.

The way by which such needs are known is through his work as a pastor. Here Gladden speaks of the minister as a friend: "He ought to be the one man in all the vicarage to whom the heart of any one in need of a friend would instinctively turn." Speaking of the pastor, he says,

As friend and counselor and guide of men, heavy responsibilities will be laid upon him. There will be no confessional in which he will sit as the mouthpiece of God, to hear the word of the penitent and pronounce absolution, but if he is the kind of man that he ought to be, a great many stories of doubt and perplexity and sorrow and shame and despair are likely to be poured into his ears. The cure of souls is his high calling; it invokes for him what tenderness, what dignity, what sympathetic insight, what sanity of judgment, what love for men, what faith in God!

There is . . . in every congregation enough of real trouble to tax the minister's resources of sympathetic wisdom. How much there is, in every community, of anxiety and disappointment and heartbreaking sorrow that never comes to the surface, of which the gossiping world knows nothing at all! A great deal of this comes to the minister; he must always be the sharer of many burdens which are hidden from the public gaze. This is just as it ought to be; the pastor has as little reason to complain of it as the doctor has to complain of a multitude of patients. But it is apt to be the most exhaustive part of the pastor's work; the drafts made upon his nervous energy through the appeal to his sympathies are heavier than those which are due to his studies.[1]

When one combines such a spirit of pastoral concern with such a spirit of dedication in preaching, results are bound to follow.

---

[1] pp. 107, 108, 109, 174, 176-178.

The
Education of Our Wants

*He that gathered much had nothing over, and
he that gathered little had no lack.*

—Exodus 16:18

THIS IS SAID concerning that marvelous bread from heaven, the manna, which fed the children of Israel in the wilderness. Every evening it lay upon the ground in small white flakes, an abundant supply of it, and they were bidden to gather it, "an omer a head, according to the number of your persons shall ye take it every man for them which are in his tent. And the children of Israel did so, and gathered—some more, some less." Some, perhaps, were greedy and feared that they would not get enough, and some were timid and withheld their hands lest they should take too much. But when they came to measure it, the communistic rule was exactly and supernaturally enforced. All had exactly the same amount. The large hoards shrank and the scanty hoards expanded; there was just an omer apiece, all round, in every tent. The greedy were no better off for their greed and the timid were no worse off for their timidity. It is the only society of which I have read, except that in Mr. Bellamy's *Looking Backward,* in which the portions of all were exactly equalized. And it would seem that the supply and the demand in every case were precisely equivalent. No one had more than he wanted: no one wanted more than he had. Wants and possessions were in perfect agreement.

This brings us to the theme which I wish to consider with you this morning—the schooling of human wants. We need a great many kinds of education—the education of our muscles, that they may be vigorous and elastic; of our nerves, that they may be at once alert and sedate; of

our senses, that they may properly mediate between ourselves and our environment; of our intellects, that they
may digest and assimilate the knowledge brought to us;
of our imaginations, that they may fashion for us cre-
ations sacred and beautiful; of our affections, that they
may cleave unto whatsoever things are pure and honest
and of good report—but not less of our wants, those imperious, insistent, inward powers that do so much to give
direction and momentum to our lives. The education of
our wants—is there anything more serious or pressing?
If every one of those who are listening to me could get
his wants properly trained and disciplined so that he
should want everything he needed and nothing that was
not good for him; so that he should want the best things
most and the things of least value least—what a happy
company this would be?

The beginning of this education of wants is the awakening of wants. Certain primary animal cravings are
present in the infant of days, but the range of instinctive
desires is comparatively narrow, and without a stimulating education does not greatly widen. The history of
civilization is the history of the awakening and multipli-
cation of human wants. The missionary finds the savages
of Africa to be creatures with very few wants. They require a little coarse food, a very little clothing, a shelter
of mud with no window and no chimney, a bow or a
spear, a hatchet of stone, some rude family life, some human attachment to the tribe or the clan, some interven-
tion, now and then, of priest or juggler with weird rites
to represent and propitiate the powers of that other world
of which the spirit must have some haunting sense; but
when you have made up your full catalogue of all the
things this primitive man ever thinks of and wishes for,
how meagre a list it is. All the elements of a man are
there; he has a body with its appetites, a mind with reasoning power, a social nature that links him with his kind,

a spirit that holds converse with the unseen—yet how little it takes to satisfy all his desire!

The first thing to do for him is to make him want more things and better things—and this is precisely the process which goes on in his life. Some of us heard one of our missionaries explaining it very vividly, not long ago. The savage by his contact with the missionary finds unconsciously awakened in him new wants. He begins to want better garments to protect him from the cold and to shield him from the sun; a better house to live in, in which the smoke of his fire will not blind and strangle him, and into which the sunlight may find its way; better food to eat; better implements—an axe and a spade and a plow; presently he wants that mysterious power of communicating with some one at a distance, which he sees the missionary exercising, when he makes marks upon a bit of paper, and it is carried to some one else in the next village who understands it and answers in the same way—magic, it seems to the wondering child of Nature, but he wants to possess it for himself and for his children; and thus his intellectual wants are awakened and he is started on the long and gainful quest of the knowledge that can be transmitted by letters and the power which such knowledge gives. By and by he learns, through his love for the man who is bringing him all these wonderful things, to listen to what the man has to tell him about the Father of us all, and the Lord and Leader of men, and finds a want springing up in his heart for the love of this all-Father and the friendship of this great Friend.

We can all see that the deepest need of this fellow creature, tied so close to the earth, is the awakening and development of new wants. The trouble with him in his native state is that he has so few desires; that he is not at all aware of the many good things that are within his reach. We can all see that the development of wants, even on the material side of his nature, is a normal and healthy process; that it is as natural and wholesome for the human nature to put forth these new cravings as for the plant to put forth new buds and branches; that we advance toward perfection by the awakening and the satisfying of new desires. It is well for the Bushman or the Hottentot that he has learned to want a garment for his nakedness, a house instead of a mud hut, a table, at which he may sit down with his wife and children, asking God's blessing on his food and making each meal a sacrament, instead of snatching a morsel here and there and eating as the wild beast eats, in solitude, with a growl at every intruder; it is well that he has learned to till his fields, and store his fruits and grains and protect himself against famine; it is well that there has been kindled in his soul that thirst for knowledge by which he has been enabled to open the treasures of the world's learning; above all, it is well that he has come to put away from his mind the deadly and paralyzing fear of things unseen, and to open his heart to the love of the Father in heaven, and to the hopes and promises of the life everlasting. We know that when our ancestors, in the German forests, or beside the British fens, were thus visited with influences from without and above themselves that kindled in them the wish for other and higher life, and led them away from barbarism toward civilization, it was well for them, and for us, their children.

From that day to this the process has been going on; the awakened intellect of man has been discovering new possibilities, new combinations of natural force, new uses of natural products, new ministries to human need, and thus has been developing and multiplying human wants. Progress consists largely in the creation and diversification of wants.

What a tremendous enterprise it has come to be—the cultivation of wants in the breasts of the children of men!

Whole armies of men are engaged in planting the seeds of wants in the minds of their neighbors. Invention largely takes this direction; infinite energy is expended by multitudes in contriving things which shall create wants. Scores of beautiful and attractive pages in our magazines, and striking displays in the columns of our newspapers are devoted to making us want things; as the swift cars bear us across the country our eyes are constantly caught by startling legends whose purpose it is to make us want something that we do not now possess. The business of advertising, which has come to be perhaps the most extensive and the most expensive business now carried on in highly civilized lands, is chiefly devoted to the stimulation and direction of human wants. The artists who arrange the shop windows and the showcases are masters in this branch of education. One cannot walk far in a city like this without coming upon something which is designed to awaken in him a want for what he does not now possess. A small girl of my acquaintance, three or four years old, on her first visit to a toy store, stood still and looked with wonder up and down the shelves and counters, and finally said, with an air of pensive surprise: "Why, *I* haven't got all these things!" The business had been done for her; the response of her nature to the appeal of the exhibitor was precisely what he sought.

The business is partly effectually done for all of us. Whatever else our enterprising captains of civilization fail to do, they do not fail in the production of wants; vast crops of them are sown and harvested every year; the supply does not quiet the demand, but stimulates it; the more we have the more we crave. If those of you who have come to maturity of years are able to take an inventory of the things you find yourselves wanting now, and to compare it with a similar inventory of the things you were wanting forty years ago, you will be surprised, perhaps, to see what an addition has been made to the number of the things regarded by you as needful. If any of you can recall your life in college forty years ago and compare your wants then with the wants of your own boys and girls now in college, you will have another illuminating illustration of the way wants multiply.

In fact, there is reason to fear that this business of creating and diversifying wants has gone quite too far in the lives of many of us. We must not quarrel with civilization, but it is hard to resist the conviction that there has been developed a vast number of unreal, superficial, artificial wants; that cravings have been kindled in many of us for much that adds nothing to life, to its strength, its beauty, its usefulness, its real satisfaction. Indeed, we must say that many of us are possessed and dominated by cravings for that which is hurtful and degrading and destructive to manhood. But, putting aside the debasing appetites, the hankerings for pollution and poison—there is still a vast number of unnatural and trivial cravings through which a large part of the vital energies of men in this generation are poured out, and which bring into the life nothing but emptiness and weariness and poverty of soul. Take the life of our frivolous plutocracy—the life of the thousands of young men and women in this country who have money to burn, as they say, and nothing to do but amuse themselves, and make a catalogue of the things which have become to them imperative wants. What a pitiful exhibit it would be!

I doubt whether a sadder, a more depressing picture was ever painted, in any age of the world, than that which is found in a few of the middle chapters of Richard Whiteing's novel, *Number Five, John Street*—his picture of the life of the rich young men of London. It is not a grossly immoral life as he shows it to us; but it is so empty, so trivial, so utterly devoid of purpose, so absorbed with inanities. Neither Horace nor Juvenal can show us anything more disheartening. Decidedly the people of the slums, between whom and these heavy swells of the West End the story vibrates, are a far more hopeful class. The sketch of Seton Ridler is too obviously a sketch from the life. Such a character could not have been invented.

The most striking and manifestly the most realistic feature of this description is the impression it gives us of the labor and weariness of this kind of life. The engagements are so multitudinous and the demands of this artificial life are so exacting that existence becomes a burden. "I tell you," says one of these devotees of fashion, "it's just like working in mosaic—so many little bits to fit in. I don't think our set ever gets a chance in life."

"Always slaving," comments his friend.

"That's it. Sometimes when I feel I can't lay hold of it all, I wish I was a 'bloke,' with four bank holidays a year, and there an end."

"And yet we are called the idle rich."

" 'Idle rich!' Where would the poor be if we struck for a quiet life? I work ten hours a day inventing wants for myself, and work for them, and very often eight hours' overtime."

Such is the congestion of wants to which our complex civilization is bringing many of those who are regarded as the favorites of fortune. It is a melancholy condition. There is no health in it for body or mind or soul—no comfort, no satisfaction; the pleasures are those of Sisyphus— always rolling the stone uphill to see it go crashing down again; the recreation it brings is like the nightmare compared with refreshing sleep.

It is a far cry from the Bushman in the African forest to the denizens of the London Mayfair, or the favorites of the New York "Four Hundred," staggering under the burden of artificial cravings. Sometimes the social philosopher, revolting from the excesses of our complex civilization, harks back to that primitive barbarism, making the gentle savage his ideal, and proposing to return to that kind of simplicity. That was Rousseau's idea, and Tolstoy seems to be of some such mind. It is a foolish counsel. The bird will not return to the egg and it is idle to talk about it. To throw away all the gains of civilization would be treachery to humanity. To propose forswearing all the new powers with which invention has equipped us, all the comforts of life, all the refinements of culture, all the pure and elevating pleasures of art, is not a sign of sanity. The barbarian with no wants is certainly quite as far from the ideal of human perfection as is the London swell, swamped beneath the burden of them. The tree needs pruning, not cutting up by the roots. It is not the extermination but the education of wants that is called for. A being without wants is a being destitute of motive power; it is not to stagnation and immobility that we wish to betake ourselves, but to simplicity and health and vigor.

What then is our problem? I think that I must have brought it pretty clearly before your minds in this descriptive sketch. The fact that confronts us is the twofold danger to which human life is exposed, on the one side to the dearth and on the other side to the plethora of wants. There are many among us who have not wants enough; who are quite too well content with squalor and stupidity and ignorance; on the other side there are too many who are so entangled and enslaved by their wants that life has ceased to have for them any high significance; their freedom and their strength are gone. It is well for us clearly to discern both these dangers, and to be on our guard against them. The awakening of new wants may be to some of us a prime necessity; the elimination of artificial and incumbering wants may be to others the first duty. The creature without desire is a clod, the creature whose life is ravaged and overrun by hoards of clamorous desires is an object of pity.

With most of us, I dare say, the danger is greatest on this side. We have too many wants. A large part of the energy of our souls is expended in hungering and thirsting after that which is not worth while. We are the slaves of cravings from which, if we could but free ourselves, we should be happier and stronger. I am not now thinking most of indulgences essentially vicious and corrupting, but of the excessive devotion to the mere externalities of life—to adornments, and amusements, and sensuous gratifications, to the lust of the eyes and the lust of the flush and the pride of life. I am sure that if the old prophet were here this morning, and knew some of you as well as I know you, you would hear him saying very earnestly: "Wherefore do you spend money for that which is not bread, and your labor for that which satisfieth not? Hearken unto me, and eat ye that which is good, and let your soul delight itself in fatness."

We must educate our wants. And the first lesson that we must teach them is that they are not our masters. The motive power of life they may be, but they are not its directing intelligence, and they must not usurp the place that does not belong to them. We will let them serve us, but they must not rule us. That is the trouble with them. "Our needs," says Charles Wagner, "in place of the servants they should be, have become a turbulent and seditious crowd, a legion of tyrants in miniature. A man enslaved to his needs may best be compared to a bear with a ring in its nose that is led about and made to dance at will. The likeness is not flattering, but you will grant that it is true." We must not be the slaves of our cravings. A mere blind want must never be our master. We must bring all these clamorous longings of ours under the rule of reason, and let them be gratified or suppressed according to its arbitration.

It is only an extension of the same idea to say that we must teach our wants to know and keep their places. They are not of equal rank; there are higher and lower, greater and less among them, and the education that they need is that which gives to each its true order and importance, which forbids the lesser to usurp the places that belong to the greater. To desire most strongly and most constantly that which is most precious and most enduring; to shake from their hold upon our hearts the legions of trivialities and vanities—this is the beginning and the end of wisdom in the schooling of our wants. To want the best things most and the poorest things least— if this were our happy state of mind how beautiful our lives would be!

And what are the best things? Plainly they are the things that belong to character—the things that pertain to ourselves, more than to our possessions and surroundings; the essential manhood and womanhood, and not its appendages of wealth or rank or decoration. The wants which lay hold on the qualities of character, that make us larger, truer, better men, these we may cultivate and stimulate all we will; there is no danger that these elements will be overdeveloped. Blessed are they that hunger and thirst after righteousness, for they shall be filled.

Men and women, there are some of you who need to lay this truth to heart. You have many wants, some more imperious than others; do they not need from you some careful schooling? Would it not be well for you to take a pretty careful inventory of them today? Find a quiet place somewhere and sit down and make an honest list of them. Think over the things that occupy your mind most constantly and enlist most fully the strength of your wishes. Get the things that you are really hungering and thirsting for clearly before your thought; then put down the things that your conduct proves to be of secondary importance, and the things that you sometimes wish for but do not greatly dwell upon. Look them over and see whether the order needs revising; whether those which are really the greatest in your estimation ought not to be the least, and those that are least ought not to be greatest.

I have no doubt that in the hearts of all of you, with some distempered and misdirected cravings are many worthy wishes. One thing, I fear, is uppermost in the desires of many, but that I will not name. It is such a cheap and common thing that we will not speak of it. Let it pass. But there are other and better things. You wish for knowledge, for skill, for capacity, for perfection in art, for a good reputation, for recognition and friendship, for the power of influencing men, and all these are worth possessing. But none of them is entitled to the first place in our affections. Surely you know that the crowning wish, the commanding wish of your life must be the wish to be right and true and sound in the centre of your life, to be right in your ruling purpose, to be right with God— to be in harmony with him in the governing principles of your life. No good that you can think of is higher than that, and you cannot get your own consent to put anything which is lower than that upon the throne of your choice. Put it there today. Come to a clear understanding with yourself that this is the principal thing, and the thing on which your heart shall henceforth be set. You hope to possess this great good some day. Register it then in your own consciousness, as your chief want, and make all the other objects of desire bow down and serve it. "It is the least that a man can do," says Canon Mozely, "to wish with all his heart that he had some valuable thing, if he is to expect some day to have it. How simple a condition, could man only resolve steadily to wish for the possession of that which he knows to be his chief good; could he but cast aside, once for all, all those vain, those fruitless longings for things that are out of his reach; for gifts and faculties which only glitter and attract the eye; and wish in the sincerity of his heart for what is really to be had for the wishing—for religious faith and temper."

It is really to be had for the wishing—this one supreme good, of friendship with God, a heart and life in harmony with his will. All we have to do is to make it the supreme wish of our hearts, and it will surely be ours. Of none of the other things that we set our hearts upon can we be sure, and we get most of them, if we get them at all, only at heavy cost:—

> For a cap and bells our lives we pay;
> 　Bubbles we buy with a whole soul's tasking;
> 'Tis heaven alone that is given away,
> 　'Tis only God may be had for the asking.

If we fail of this highest good, it is only because we do not strongly wish for it, because we suffer some lesser good to supplant this upon the throne of our desire. "Ye shall seek me and find me when ye shall search for me with all your hearts, saith the Lord."